Institute of Biology's
Studies in Biology no. 14

KU-549-990

Plants and Water

Second Edition

James F. Sutcliffe

D.Sc., Ph.D., F.I.Biol.

Professor of Plant Physiology,
University of Sussex

Edward Arnold

© J. F. Sutcliffe, 1979

First published 1968
by Edward Arnold (Publishers) Limited,
41 Bedford Square, London WC1B 3DQ

Reprinted 1969, 1971, 1973, 1974, 1976

Second edition 1979
Reprinted 1986

Edward Arnold (Australia) Pty Ltd,
80 Waverley Road,
Caulfield East,
Victoria 3145,
Australia

Edward Arnold,
3 East Read Street,
Baltimore,
Maryland 21202,
USA

HERTFORDSHIRE
LIBRARY SERVICE
N.F.

British Library Cataloguing in Publication Data

Sutcliffe, James
    Plants and water. – 2nd ed. – (Institute of Biology.
    Studies in biology; no. 14 ISSN 0537-9024).
    1. Plant-water relationships
    I. Title   II. Series
    581.1$'$9$'$212   QK870

ISBN: 0-7131-2751-1

All rights reserved. No part of this publication
may be reproduced, stored in a retrieval system,
or transmitted, in any form or by any means, electronic,
mechanical, photocopying, recording or otherwise, without
the prior permission of Edward Arnold (Publishers) Ltd.

Printed and bound in Great Britain at
The Camelot Press Ltd, Southampton

COUNTY PLANNING
AND ESTATES
DEPARTMENT
TECHNICAL LIBRARY

General Preface to the Series

Because it is no longer possible for one textbook to cover the whole field of biology while remaining sufficiently up to date, the Institute of Biology has sponsored this series so that teachers and students can learn about significant developments. The enthusiastic acceptance of 'Studies in Biology' shows that the books are providing authoritative views of biological topics.

The features of the series include the attention given to methods, the selected list of books for further reading and, wherever possible, suggestions for practical work.

Readers' comments will be welcomed by the Education Officer of the Institute.

1979   Institute of Biology
                                                                41 Queen's Gate
                                                                London SW7 5BR

Preface to the Second Edition

During the past ten years, the water potential terminology advocated in the first edition of this study has been adopted widely by plant physiologists. It is slowly making its appearance in school textbooks and examination syllabi, and now that its advantages have been established, the sooner it is employed universally the better.

Research in the field of plant water relations continues actively, and to take account of new developments parts of the booklet have been extended for this new edition. An attempt has been made to incorporate the many helpful suggestions that have been offered by readers, and in response to a number of requests, a subject index and glossary have been included.

I am grateful to Dr J. E. Dale, Mr P. W. Freeland and Dr D. G. Pope for their helpful comments on the draft manuscript and to many others, including students, who have supplied me with information and advice. My sincere thanks are also due to those who have kindly agreed to allow me to use published material; to Miss Nora Browning, who typed the manuscript; and to my wife, Janet Ann, and the staff of Edward Arnold, Ltd, for all their help.

1979   J. F. S.

Contents

the xylem   6.3 Mechanism of water movement in the xylem
6.4 Availability of soil water   6.5 Absorption of water by roots
6.6 Root pressure and guttation   6.7 Transport of water in the
phloem   6.8 Effects of water stress on physiological processes

Plants and water.

1 Plants and Water

1.1 Water requirement

The devastating drought in the British Isles during the summer of 1976, which was the worst for at least 250 years, and the recent long dry spell in the western United States have served to focus attention again on the importance of water for plant and animal life. In other parts of the world, notably North Africa and the Middle East, water conservation for agricultural and domestic purposes is an ever-present problem. It has been estimated that an herbaceous plant, such as a sunflower, when plentifully supplied with water may absorb through its roots, several times its own volume of water on a hot summer's day, while a forest of deciduous trees in temperate latitudes may consume annually as much as the equivalent of 50 cm of rain.

Most of the water that is taken up by a plant is lost again by evaporation from the leaves, a process which is known as transpiration. An American plant physiologist, E. C. Miller, has calculated that maize plants (*Zea mays*) transpire over 98% of all the water they absorb. Most of the rest is retained in the plant tissues, and only a minute proportion ($\simeq 0.2\%$) is used in photosynthesis (Fig. 1–1).

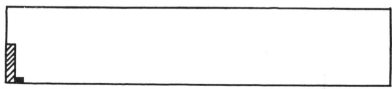

Fig. 1–1 Relative amounts of water transpired (clear area), retained (shaded), and consumed (black) by maize (*Zea mays*) plants. (Data from MILLER, 1938.)

These proportions are probably fairly representative of many crop plants, e.g. cereals and legumes, growing in moderately dry air with adequate irrigation. Even desert plants (xerophytes – see below) transpire a high proportion (at least 50%) of the water they absorb. Submerged aquatic plants (hydrophytes) retain a much larger part of the water taken up than other plants although the amounts they absorb are smaller.

1.2 Water content

Of all the substances absorbed by plants from their environment, water is obviously required in the largest amount. It is also the most abundant constituent of plants, sometimes comprising as much as 95% of the total mass. Only in woody tissues and in dormant organs does the water content fall much below 80%, but in some dry seeds it may be as low as 5% (Table 1). The mature seeds of some plants (e.g. *Amaryllis* and *Crinum* spp.) have a high water content (usually over 70%) and this enables them to germinate without an external water supply.

Table 1   Water contents of various plant parts expressed as percentages of fresh mass (FM) and dry mass (DM).

Plant	Part	Water content as a percentage of FM	DM
Lettuce (*Lactuca sativa*)	young leaf	94.3	1654
Water melon (*Citrullus vulgaris*)	ripe fruit	92.6	1251
Carrot (*Daucus carota*)	mature root	90.3	931
Strawberry (*Fragaria chiloensis*)	ripe fruit	89.1	817
Potato (*Solanum tuberosum*)	tuber	79.8	395
Iris (*Iris* cv 'Wedgwood')	bulb	62.0	163
Coconut (*Cocos nucifera*)	solid endosperm	50.9	104
Barley (*Hordeum vulgare*)	dry grain	10.2	11.4
Peanut (*Arachis hypogaea*)	seed	5.2	5.5

The usual method of determining water content is to dry the material in an oven until it attains constant mass. Care must be taken to avoid charring, which is an indication of loss of dry matter, and for this reason relatively low temperatures (< 85°C) are usually employed. A small amount of water associated with the organic substances ('bound' water) is not removed by this procedure. Water content can be expressed as a percentage of either fresh or dry mass (Table 1); the former basis is commonly used, but the latter is sometimes preferable, especially when water content is high, since in such cases large variations in the amount of water present cause rather small changes in water content expressed as a percentage of fresh mass. On the other hand, water content represented as a percentage of dry mass can sometimes be misleading, because if the dry mass changes, e.g. as a result of accumulation or depletion of storage products, water content per unit of dry matter will change when the actual amount of water present remains constant.

The water content of a plant is very variable and it changes markedly with fluctuations in soil moisture content and the humidity of the air. In most cases, transpiration exceeds water absorption during most of the day so that water content decreases, while the situation is reversed at night (Fig. 1–2). Thus in effect a plant replenishes in its tissues during the night, water that was lost the previous day. In cacti, e.g. *Opuntia*, however, where the stomata close during the day the opposite occurs (Fig. 1–2). Similarly,

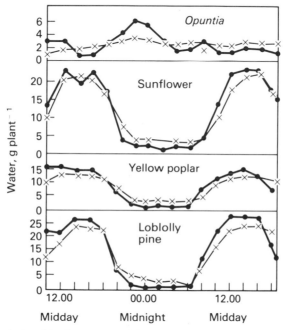

Fig. 1–2   Relationship between water absorption and transpiration in four dissimilar plants growing in well watered soil on a summer's day. Absorption (x——x), transpiration (●——●). (After KRAMER, 1969.)

the water content of the trunk of a deciduous tree in temperate regions rises during the winter when transpiration is low and decreases in the summer when it is high. This has important consequences for the forestry industry when timber is being floated down rivers, as waterlogged wood is more dense than that in which water has been partly replaced by air.

Relative water content (RWC) is the amount of water in a tissue compared with the amount the tissue will hold without infiltration of intercellular air spaces. The RWC of a leaf is measured by weighing it fresh (FM_1) and then floating it on water in an enclosed space for about 24 hours, preferably in the light, and weighing it again (FM_2) after wiping off superfluous water. The dry mass (DM) is then determined as described above and RWC calculated from the formula:

$$RWC = \frac{FM_1 - DM}{FM_2 - DM}$$

Thus the maximum value of RWC is unity; often, RWC is expressed as a percentage of maximum water content by multiplying the value obtained from the above formula by 100. Water saturation deficit (WSD) is a term which is sometimes applied to the difference between RWC expressed as a percentage, and 100, that is:

$$WSD = 100 - RWC \ (\%)$$

The water content of some plants, notably lichens and bryophytes, is affected by environmental conditions much more than is that of others. In such 'poikilohydrous' plants, which exert little or no control over water loss, water content is closely correlated with atmospheric humidity, and RWC may vary by as much as 90%.

1.3   Functions of water

Living organisms are believed to have originated in an aqueous environment and in the course of evolution they have exploited the properties of water in a number of ways. The major uses of water in plants may be summarized as follows:

(i) Water is an essential constituent of protoplasm, often comprising more than 90% of its total mass. Most biological molecules are hydrated in their natural state and the presence of water is essential for maintenance of their structure and activity. When protoplasm is dehydrated gradually, as during the development of seeds, its rate of metabolism decreases and it becomes dormant (see VILLIERS, 1975). If water is removed too quickly protoplasm is killed because rapid dehydration can lead to irreversible denaturation of proteins.

(ii) Water participates directly in a number of chemical reactions occurring in living material. Hydrolytic and condensation reactions in which water is added to or removed from organic molecules are important in various metabolic processes, such as the interconversion of carbohydrates, e.g.

$$(C_6H_{10}O_5)n + nH_2O \rightleftharpoons nC_6H_{12}O_6$$
$$\text{starch} \qquad\qquad\qquad \text{glucose}$$

or the synthesis of malic acid from fumaric acid in the Krebs cycle:

$$HOOC.CH = CH.COOH + H_2O \rightleftharpoons HOOC.CH_2\, CHOH.COOH$$

fumaric acid   malic acid
(*trans*-butanedioic acid)   (2-hydroxybutanedioic acid)

(iii) Water is a source of protons (H^+ ions) for the reduction of carbon dioxide in photosynthesis, and of hydroxyl (OH^-) ions which provide electrons for the light reactions:

$$H_2O \rightleftharpoons H^+ + OH^-$$

$$CO_2 + H_2O \rightleftharpoons [CH_2O] + O_2$$
$$\text{carbohydrate}$$

(iv) Water is the solvent in which many other substances are dissolved and in which they undergo chemical reactions in protoplasm.

(v) Water is also the solvent in which materials are transported in the xylem and phloem and probably also through the cytoplasm of cells (see Chapter 6, and RICHARDSON, 1975).

(vi) Much of the water in a plant is contained in large vacuoles within the cytoplasm of parenchyma cells (Fig. 3-1, p. 29). This water helps to maintain the rigidity (turgidity) of cells (see Chapter 3), and hence of the plant as a whole. When cells lose their turgidity the plant droops or wilts and stops growing.

(vii) Gains and losses of water from plant cell vacuoles are responsible for a variety of movements in plants, including the opening and closing of stomata (Chapter 4); the nocturnal folding of the leaflets of leguminous plants, such as acacias, and the opening and closing of flowers in response to temperature (see SUTCLIFFE, 1977).

(viii) There is a thin layer of water surrounding each cell of a plant and this permeates the micro-spaces between solid material in cell walls. These surface films are continuous from cell to cell throughout the plant and are important both in the diffusion of gases (CO_2 and O_2) into and out of cells, and in the uptake and transport of mineral salts from the soil by roots (see SUTCLIFFE and BAKER, 1974).

(ix) Because of its high specific heat (see Chapter 2) water acts as a heat sink and makes it possible for plants to absorb a large amount of solar radiation without an injurious rise in temperature. Furthermore, as the evaporation of water has a high latent heat, transpiration has a powerful cooling effect which helps a plant to dissipate heat absorbed as solar radiation (see Chapter 5 and SUTCLIFFE, 1977).

(x) Water is the medium through which motile gametes effect fertilization, either in the external environment as in the case of lower plants, or internally through the pollen tube of seed plants. Water also assists in various ways in the dissemination of spores, fruits and seeds. The drying of some fruits leads to the development of tensions in the tissues which cause explosive dehiscence and dispersal of seeds.

(xi) In submerged, or partly submerged, aquatic plants, external water provides support because of the buoyancy of stems and leaves. Such plants have poorly developed strengthening tissues (see below).

1.4   Influence of water supply on plant structure and distribution

The availability of water in the environment has an important effect on plant distribution both on a world-wide basis (see Table 2) and at a more local level. Plants which are adapted to grow in dry places cannot survive for long in wet habitats and vice versa. Individual species are classified into one of four groups on the basis of the amount of water available to them and each group is characterized by a combination of structural adaptations to their environment.

Hydrophytes grow either fully immersed in water, or partially submerged. They include marine algae such as seaweeds, and the submerged angiosperm eel-grass (*Zostera marina*), which are also adapted to withstand high salinity (that is, they are *halophytes*). Other examples of hydrophytes are the fresh water aquatics ranging from motile unicellular algae, such as *Chlamydomonas*, to free floating ferns, e.g. *Azolla filiculoides*, and angiosperms, e.g. duckweed (*Lemna minor*). Some emergent hydrophytes, such as the water-lilies (*Nymphaea alba* and *Nuphar lutea*), and mare's-tail (*Hippuris vulgaris*) and many seaweeds are firmly anchored to the substratum so that they are not easily carried away by water currents. The submerged leaves of water plants are often finely divided (e.g. in *Myriophyllum* spp.) and this reduces resistance to water flow.

Water loss is not usually a problem for hydrophytes and there is no well-developed cuticle on submerged organs or on the under-surface of floating leaves. The upper surface on the other hand is heavily cutinized, which helps to prevent water-logging, and emergent leaves also have functional stomata which control transpiration.

Hydrophytes usually have poorly-developed xylem and their support comes mainly from the surrounding water. There are extensive air spaces which increase the buoyancy and facilitate diffusion of oxygen and CO_2 through the tissues (Fig. 1–3). An additional problem for submerged hydrophytes is that the light intensity to which they are exposed is relatively low, and they are adapted to photosynthesize efficiently under these conditions. Hydrophytes do not usually survive desiccation except when they are in a dormant state; the floating leaves of *Chamaegigas intrepidus*, a minute water plant of South Africa, can withstand drying by equilibration with air at 5% relative humidity when they are folded in the bud whereas they are killed if the air is dryer than 95% relative humidity when they are mature (GAFF, 1971).

Hygrophytes, e.g. many mosses and liverworts, and some ferns, are land plants which inhabit damp situations where the air is usually highly humid and the soil often saturated with water. Such habitats are generally shaded and so hygrophytes are adapted to photosynthesize efficiently at low light intensities. They commonly have a large surface area in relation to volume and leaves are often only a single layer of cells thick. There is little control of water loss and water content is governed largely by the

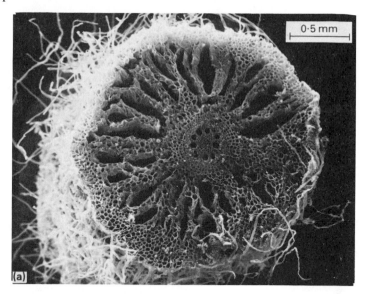

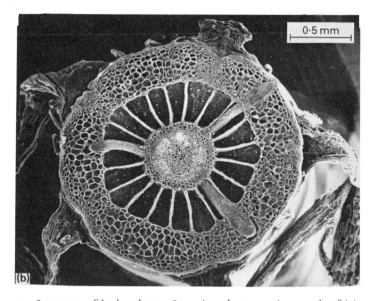

Fig. 1–3 Structure of hydrophytes. Scanning electron micrograph of (a) root of *Typha* sp. Note the large air spaces which are continuous with those of the stem and numerous root hairs. (b) Stem of *Myriophyllum brasilense* cut at a node showing large air spaces in the cortex and development of adventitious roots from the central stele. (Photographs reproduced by courtesy of Dr J. M. Bristow, Queens University, Kingston, Canada.)

Table 2   The main climatic zones and types of natural vegetation.

Climatic zone	Vegetation type
1 *Wet tropical:* hot with heavy rainfall throughout the year	Tropical rain forest
2 *Dry tropical:* winter hot and dry; summer hot and wet	Monsoon forest Savannah
3 *Desert:* no regular rainfall; wide range of temperature	Desert scrub (cacti, etc.; ephemerals)
4 *Semi-arid:* winter dry, summer hot with early rain	Prairie (long grass) Steppe (short grass)
5 *Humid-temperate:* winter warm and wet; summer hot and dry	Sub-tropical forest (mainly evergreen)
6 *Mediterranean:* winter cool with moderate rainfall; summer hot and dry	Mediterranean scrub (olive, citrus, agave, etc.)
7 *Cool temperate:* winter cool; summer warm; rainfall throughout the year	Broad-leaved forest (mainly deciduous)
8 *Continental:* winter cold; summer hot; rainfall variable	Mixed and coniferous forest Boreal forest (talgo)
9 *Arctic:* winter very cold; summer short, cold and dry	Tundra (mosses, lichens, low shrubs)
10 *Montane:* winter very cold; summer short; temperature and rainfall variable	Alpine (mosses, lichens, low shrubs)

humidity of the air (see above). Many hygrophytes can withstand prolonged desiccation and begin to grow again as soon as water is supplied.

Mesophytes are plants which normally grow in well-drained soils and whose leaves are exposed to moderately dry air. Most crop species and many of the native plants of temperate and tropical regions come into this category. They have an impermeable cuticle and regulate water-loss by controlling the size of the stomata (see Chapter 4). In mesophytes the stomata often close for a period in the middle of the day when conditions are generally most favourable for evaporation, and also at night when photosynthesis is stopped, and uptake of CO_2 is not required. As mesophytes have to replace large quantities of water transpired by the leaves, they have an extensive root system and well-developed xylem. Many perennial mesophytes are deciduous, shedding their leaves to conserve water when conditions are unfavourable, e.g. during winter in temperate and arctic latitudes and during dry seasons in the tropics. The above-ground parts of some herbaceous mesophytes die down completely at such times and the plants survive by underground perennating organs such as rhizomes, bulbs or corms.

Xerophytes occur mainly in deserts, dry grasslands and in rocky places where water is generally scarce. They will sometimes, although not always, grow better in moister than in dryer places if they are protected from competition with mesophytes. Their survival under drought conditions depends on a number of adaptations, including:

(i) An extensive root system which penetrates widely and deeply in the soil to obtain such water as is available. The cells of these roots have exceptionally low water potentials (see below) which enables them to absorb water from very dry soil.

(ii) Water may be stored in swollen ('succulent') roots, stems or leaves for use during periods of severe drought. The ice plant (*Mesembryanthemum crystallinum*) has enlarged bladder-like epidermal cells on the leaves which act as water stores. The development of succulence in leaves and stems leads to a reduction in the ratio of surface area to volume which helps to reduce water loss. An extreme situation occurs in the so-called 'pebble' or 'stone' plants (*Lithops* spp.) in which the leaves, borne close to the ground on short stems, are rounded or club shaped, resembling stones.

(iii) In many xerophytes, including cacti, the leaves are reduced in size, sometimes to mere scales, and the main photosynthetic organ is the stem. This is often flattened and leaf-like in appearance. An interesting example of evolutionary reversion is seen in such plants as the butcher's broom (*Ruscus aculeatus*) where the true leaves are reduced to scales and portions of the stem expanded into leaf-like structures called cladodes. The central region of a cladode is occupied by large water-storing cells. A similar modification occurs in species of *Acacia* where the leaf blade is reduced and a flattened expanded petiole (phyllode) takes its place.

(iv) Some xerophytes especially monocotyledons shed their leaves and other above-ground parts in times of severe drought and survive by means of underground bulbs and corms. The creosote bush (*Covillea glutinosa*) of North American deserts has small leathery leaves which, when a drought occurs, go brown and dry out until their water content falls to less than 10% normal. In this condition, when most leaves would die, they can remain alive for months and when water becomes available they expand rapidly, become green again and photosynthesize (cf. hygrophytes).

(v) The cuticle of xerophytes is often thicker than in mesophytes, but its impermeability to water depends mainly on its composition which includes a high proportion of cutin and other waxes. Many xerophytes have a dense coating of hairs or scales but these do not interrupt the continuity of the cuticle or increase its permeability. By creating a layer of still air round the plant it is argued that hairs reduce transpiration (see Chapter 5). By reflecting light they help to minimize the increase in temperature caused by solar radiation (see SUTCLIFFE, 1977).

(vi) Transpiration is also reduced in xerophytes by the number, arrangement and mode of functioning of stomata. The number of stomata per unit of surface area of leaf or stem is usually lower than in mesophytes and the pores are often (but not always) smaller. Some xerophytes have stomata that are sunk in pits, or in troughs between ridges on the leaf surface, and this is said to reduce transpiration by creating a region of still air above each stoma. It is also possible that the guard cells of sunken stomata being closer to photosynthetic cells are more responsive to changes in CO_2 levels in the intercellular spaces (see Chapter 4). Likewise, it has been argued that the significance of the rolling of the leaves of xerophytic grasses, e.g. marram grass (*Ammophila arenaria*) is to increase the concentration of CO_2 in the vicinity of the guard cells rather than to trap moist air.

The stomata of most xerophytes open for a shorter period during the day than do those of mesophytes. In some succulent plants, e.g. species of *Crassula* and *Opuntia*, they open during the night when the plants assimilate CO_2 by reactions which do not involve light energy, forming organic acids, such as malic acid (Crassulacean Acid Metabolism). These acids are converted to sugars in the light with release of CO_2 which can be used for photosynthesis even though the stomata are closed.

There has been much discussion as to whether halophytic angiosperms, such as glasswort (*Salicornia* spp.) and the sea blite (*Suaeda maritima*) which inhabit salt marshes, are also xerophytes. They share with xerophytes the succulent habit and large thin-walled water storage cells have been identified in the leaves. The plant geographer, Schimper, suggested that such plants may suffer from 'physiological drought' even when water is abundant in the soil because of the high concentration of salt. However, it has been shown that the cell sap of halophytes is correspondingly more concentrated and so the entry of water by osmosis (see Chapter 3) should not be impeded. Nevertheless, it is likely that some halophytes, especially those that inhabit the upper zones of salt marshes and sand dunes are exposed to periods of severe drought and it is probably for this reason that water-storing cells are often present. When water is available the rate of transpiration per unit of surface area is not very different in halophytes from that of mesophytes (DELF, 1911).

2 Physical Chemistry of Water

2.1 The structure of water

When two hydrogen atoms and an oxygen atom combine to form water, electrons are shared between them in such a way that the resulting molecule is stable and unreactive. Although the molecule as a whole is electrically-neutral, the asymmetrical distribution of electrons causes one side of the molecule to be positively charged with respect to the other (Fig. 2–1a). Such molecules, which are termed 'dipoles' tend to orientate themselves in an electrical field in such a way that the negative side lies towards the positive pole and vice versa.

Electrostatic attraction between a positively-charged region of one molecule and a negatively-charged region of a neighbouring one causes formation of a 'hydrogen' bond. These are relatively weak forces (about 20 kJ per mole of H-bonds), but nevertheless they cause water molecules to arrange themselves into a more or less ordered structure in the liquid and solid state. Because of the presence of two protons (H^+) and two lone pairs of electrons ($\ominus$) in a water molecule, each can form up to four hydrogen bonds with surrounding molecules. The bonds are arranged tetrahedrally and so molecules in ice form a regular tetrahedral crystalline structure (Fig. 2–1b). In liquid water, the molecules are more irregularly arranged than in ice and there are fewer hydrogen bonds, but some crystallinity remains (Fig. 2–1c). The heat of fusion of water suggests that about 85% of the hydrogen bonds present in ice remain intact in liquid water at 0°C and some are present even at boiling point. Thus, the chemical formula of water in the solid and liquid states, commonly expressed as H_2O, is more appropriately represented by $(H_2O)_n$ where n decreases with increase in temperature.

There are two divergent views about the structure of liquid water. X-ray studies of water at low temperature (1.5°C) have indicated that it consists of a network of hydrogen-bonded molecules enclosing large cavities filled with more-or-less disorientated molecules. Alternatively, the bonded water molecules may form short-lived clusters ('flickering clusters') embedded in a matrix of unbonded molecules. FRANKS and GOOD (1966) have suggested that both types of structure exist – the lattice predominating at low temperature and the clusters at temperatures above about 35°C.

So far it has been assumed that water consists of molecules composed entirely of the isotopes ^1H and ^{16}O. In fact, natural water also contains small amounts of the hydrogen isotopes, deuterium (^2H) and tritium (^3H), and the oxygen isotopes (^{17}O and ^{18}O). If deuterium replaces both of the

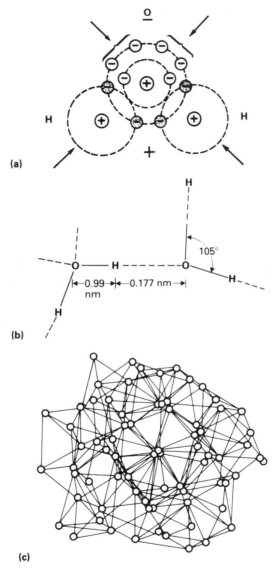

Fig. 2–1   (a) Diagrammatic representation of the structure of a water molecule showing 'shared' (stippled) and 'lone pairs' (bracketed) of electrons; arrows indicate the position of hydrogen bonds. H = hydrogen; O = oxygen. (b) Diagram showing bond angles and distances between hydrogen and oxygen atoms in ice. Covalent bonds are shown by continuous lines and hydrogen bonds as dotted lines (1 nm = 10^{-9}m). (c) Structural model of liquid water derived from computer analysis. (After BERNAL, 1965.)

hydrogen atoms the result is deuterium oxide or 'heavy' water, which has a molecular mass of twenty. Of the isotopes present in water molecules only tritium is radioactive. It is formed in the atmosphere through the action of cosmic rays and has a half life of about 12.5 years. It gets incorporated into water largely as a result of the respiration of animals and plants.

Water dissociates to a slight extent into hydronium (H_3O^+) and hydroxyl (OH^-) ions:

$$2H_2O \rightleftharpoons H_3O^+ + OH^-$$

The hydronium ion is a hydrated proton $(H^+ + H_2O)$; it is usually represented simply as H^+ and termed a hydrogen ion, or proton. The dissociation of water then becomes the familiar:

$$H_2O \rightleftharpoons H^+ + OH^-$$

At equilibrium the product of the concentrations of hydrogen ions and hydroxyl ions in pure water is constant and has a value of 10^{-14} gram-ions per dm^3. Since the total number of hydrogen ions in a given volume of pure water is exactly equal to the number of hydroxyl ions each has a concentration of 10^{-7} gram-ions per dm^3. pH is defined as the negative logarithm of hydrogen ion concentration $(pH = -\log[H^+])$ and therefore pure water has a pH value of 7. The pH value of an aqueous solution may be influenced by the presence of dissolved substances. Solutions in which the hydrogen ion concentration is greater than 10^{-7} gram ions per dm^3 $(pH < 7)$ are acidic, whereas those in which the H^+ concentration is lower than this $(pH > 7)$ are alkaline. Buffered-solutions are those in which the dissociation of a dissolved substance, e.g. a weak acid or alkali alters with pH in such a way that the solution maintains a fairly constant pH value.

2.2   Physical properties of water

Water is such a familiar substance that its unique physical properties are often taken for granted. No one is surprised that water is liquid at ordinary temperatures until its melting point and boiling point are compared with that of other substances of similar molecular size (Table 3).

From such a comparison it is evident that water has an unexpectedly high melting point and boiling point. This is attributable to association of water molecules through hydrogen bonding. If this were not the case, water would be gaseous at normal temperatures and life as we know it on earth would not be possible.

The specific heat of liquid water (Table 4) is the highest of any known substance which means that it is relatively slow to heat up and to cool down. Because plant tissues often have such a high water content (Table 1)

Table 3   Some physical constants of water and other hydrides of similar mass.

Substance	Chemical formula	Molecular mass	Melting point (°C)	Boiling point (°C)
Methane	CH_4	16	−184	−161
Ammonia	NH_3	17	−78	−33
Water	H_2O	18	0	+100
Hydrogen fluoride	HF	20	−92	+19
Hydrogen sulphide	H_2S	34	−86	−61

Table 4   Some physical constants of pure water.

Specific heat	$(J\,g^{-1})^*$	4.18	
Latent heat of melting	$(J\,g^{-1})$	334	
Heat of vaporization	$(J\,g^{-1})$	2462	(15°C)
		2253	(100°C)
Saturation vapour pressure	$(Pa)^{**}$	1.7×10	(15°C)
Density	$(kg\,dm^{-3})$	0.9991	(15°C)
		1.0000	(4°C)
		0.9999	(0°C)
Density of saturated vapour	$(kg\,dm^{-3})$	12.85×10^{-6}	
Surface tension	$(Nm^{-1})^{***}$	7.34×10^{-2}	
Viscosity	$(Pa\,s^{-1})$	1.0	(20°C)
Tensile strength	(Nm^{-2})	28×10^9	
Thermal conductivity	$(J\,m^{-1}\,s^{-1}\,{}^{\circ}K^{-1})$	0.595	
Dielectric constant		80.2	(20°C)

* The unit of energy is the Joule: its dimensions are $kg\,m^2\,s^{-2}$. 1 calorie = 4.184 J = 4.184×10^7 ergs.

** The unit of pressure is the Pascal (Pa): its dimensions are $kg\,m^{-1}\,s^{-2}$ (1 Pa = 1 Nm^{-2}), 100 kPa = 1 bar = 0.987 atmospheres.

*** The unit of force is the Newton (N): its dimensions are $kg\,m\,s^{-2}$; 10^{-5} N = 1 dyne = 1 erg cm^{-1}.

bulky organs such as tubers do not undergo rapid changes of temperature in response to changes in the environment.

The latent heat of melting and heat of vaporization of water are also unusually high. The value of 334 J g^{-1} for the latent heat of melting shows that about the same amount of heat is required to convert ice to water at 0°C as to raise the temperature of the resulting liquid to 80°C. The significance of this for plants is that a relatively large amount of heat must be extracted from water before it freezes. Similarly the evaporation of water requires a great deal of energy. For every gram of water evaporated at 15°C a leaf loses 2462 J of heat energy, and so transpiration has a powerful cooling effect.

Most liquids contract on cooling, reaching maximum density at freezing point, but water is unusual in having a maximum density at 4°C (see Table 4). For this reason, water rarely freezes solid in the sea or in deep lakes, even in the arctic. When the temperature of the deeper water falls below 4°C the water rises as its density falls, and ice forms at the surface. This insulates the water below and prevents it from being cooled down to freezing point.

At a free water surface, water molecules become orientated in such a way that most of the hydrogen bonds point inwards towards the bulk of the liquid. This confers on water its remarkably high surface tension which is higher than that on any other liquid except mercury. Surface tension is responsible for the formation of water droplets on leaves after rain, or as dew, and prevents water from entering the intercellular spaces of a leaf through open stomata. The presence of inorganic salts in the water does not have much effect on surface tension, but substances, e.g. fatty acids and certain lipids, which become concentrated at a water surface greatly reduce surface tension. Such 'surfactant' molecules have a hydrophilic ('polar') head and a hydrophobic ('non-polar') tail, and they become orientated at a water surface with the polar heads immersed in the solution and the non-polar tail protruding. Such molecules are often added to herbicide and fungicide sprays to assist in the penetration of the solution through stomata.

Water molecules adhere to surfaces such as glass as a result of electrical forces, and this property, together with high surface tension causes capillarity. Water will rise in a glass tube, .03 mm in diameter, by capillarity to a height of about 120 cm (4 feet). Capillary rise stops when the weight of the water column balances the forces of surface tension and adhesion. Water moves extensively by capillarity in the narrow spaces between soil particles, and in plant cell walls. Intermolecular forces give water a high tensile strength when it is confined in a narrow tube and so a column of water can be lifted by a force applied at the top. This is believed to be important in the ascent of sap in the xylem of plant stems (see Chapter 6).

Despite its high tensile strength water has a relatively low viscosity, that is the molecules of water slide over one another relatively easily and as a result water flows readily through narrow capillaries especially at high temperature. Raising the temperature of water from 5°C to 35°C reduces its viscosity by about 50%.

It is of considerable importance to plants that liquid water is almost colourless. The high transmission of visible light makes it possible for aquatic plants to photosynthesize at considerable depths and for light to penetrate into deeply-seated tissues of a leaf. Water absorbs light to some extent, particularly at the red end of the spectrum, and this accounts for the blue-green colour of light transmitted through a layer of water. There is a strong absorption in the infra-red which makes water a relatively good heat insulator but its thermal conductivity is still high compared with other liquids.

The dielectric constant for water is much higher than for other common liquids and this is associated with the great capacity of water to dissolve polar substances (see below).

From the above, it appears that water is ideally suited for its role in plants. This is true because plants have evolved in such a way that they can exploit to the greatest advantage the unique properties of water.

2.3   Properties of aqueous solutions

Water has been called the 'universal solvent' because it dissolves a greater variety of substances than any other liquid. The solubility of polar substances such as sucrose, which do not ionize in water, depends on hydrogen bonding between the molecules and water. Substances such as sodium chloride, which dissociate in aqueous solution into charged ions, dissolve because a shell of orientated water molecules is formed round each ion. The thickness of the hydration shell depends on the density of electrical charge in a particular ion and is greater for small ions than for larger ones carrying the same quantity of electrical charge (Fig. 2–2d). This shell acts as an electrical insulation which decreases the attraction between oppositely-charged ions and keeps them separate from one another. Nevertheless the degree of dissociation of electrolytes decreases markedly with increasing concentration, as is shown by measurements of osmotic potential (see below p. 25). Many non-polar substances (e.g. hydrocarbons) dissolve in water to a limited extent because of intermolecular attractive forces referred to as van der Waal's forces which arise from small shifts in the distribution of electrons within the molecules and increase the affinity between solute and solvent.

The physical properties of water are markedly affected by the presence of dissolved substances. This is due not only to the properties of the solute itself but to changes induced in the structure of water. For example, the freezing point is depressed and the boiling point elevated in proportion to the amount of solute added. Most solutes lower the temperature at which water attains its maximum density, but some substances, e.g. certain alcohols, increase it. The electrical conductivity of water is largely determined by the concentration of dissolved ions. For quantitative information about the physical properties of aqueous solutions the books by HARNED and OWEN (1957) and by ROBINSON and STOKES (1959) should be consulted.

The diffusion coefficient of sucrose in water at 25°C is about 0.52×10^{-9} m^2 s^{-1} whereas for common inorganic salts the values range from about 1.25×10^{-9} m^2 s^{-1} for magnesium chloride to 2.23×10^{-9} m^2 s^{-1} for

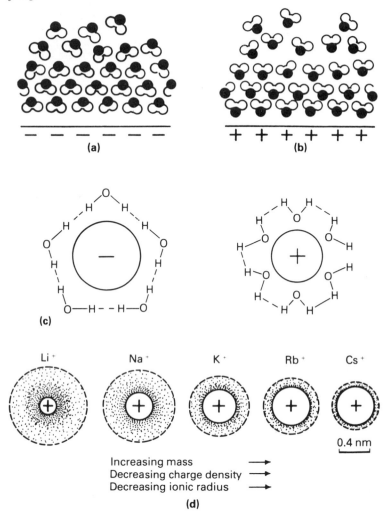

Fig. 2-2 (a) and (b) Orientation of water molecules at charged surfaces. The black circles indicate the position of oxygen atoms. (c) Arrangement of water molecules at the surface of a charged particle such as an ion. Hydrogen bonds are shown by dashed lines. (d) Relative size of hydrated alkali-metal cations. The stippled areas represent the shell of water molecules round each ion.

potassium chloride. The diffusion coefficients of these substances decrease with increasing concentration.

As Table 5 shows carbon dioxide is much more soluble in water than are oxygen and nitrogen. This is attributable to the formation of carbonic acid which dissociates into soluble hydrogen and bicarbonate ions.

$$CO_2 + H_2O \rightleftharpoons H_2CO_3 \rightleftharpoons H^+ + HCO_3^-$$

The low solubility of oxygen in water necessitates the presence of intercellular air spaces within plant tissues to ensure adequate aeration. However, the diffusion coefficient of oxygen in water (2.9×10^{-9} m^2 s^{-1} at $25°C$) is higher than that of CO_2 (1.7×10^{-7} m^2 s^{-1} at $20°C$).

Table 5   Solubility of various gases in water (mol dm^{-3} x $^{-4}$).

Gas	\multicolumn{5}{c}{$T (°C)$}
	0	10	15	20	30
CO_2	764	514	431	365	267
N_2	10.2	8.4	7.6	6.8	5.6
O_2	2.2	1.7	1.4	1.3	1.0

2.4   Water movement

2.4.1   Bulk flow

Substances move spontaneously in a physical system if their energy content is thereby decreased, that is the 'entropy' or disorderliness of the system is increased. Thus water flows downhill under the influence of gravity and in the process potential energy is converted into kinetic energy, which is dissipated as heat. Such movement carries along dissolved substances and suspended particles with it and is termed 'bulk flow', or 'mass flow'. If two vessels A and B, one containing water and the other empty, are connected by a pipe, as shown in Fig. 2–3, water will flow from A into B when the tap, T, is opened until its level in the two containers is the same. The rate of volume flow, dv/dt, depends on the hydrostatic pressure difference, ΔP, and on the resistance, R, offered by the connecting pipes, thus:

$$\frac{dv}{dt} = \frac{\Delta P}{R}$$

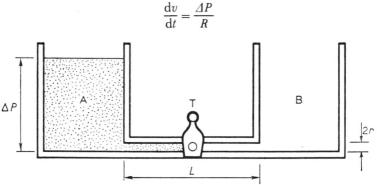

Fig. 2–3   Mass flow. For explanation, see text.

This relationship is similar to that which exists between current, voltage and resistance in an electrical circuit as is summarized by the well-known Ohm's law:

$$\text{current} = \frac{\text{voltage}}{\text{resistance}}$$

In the example given, R depends on the length of the connecting pipe L, its radius, r, and the viscosity of water, η. For relatively slow rates of flow in narrow tubes:

$$R = \frac{8\eta L}{\pi r^4}$$

and therefore,

$$\frac{dv}{dt} = \frac{\Delta p\pi r^4}{8\eta L} \qquad \text{(Poiseuille's equation)}$$

In so-called laminar flow, which obeys the Poiseuille equation, the liquid is actually stationary close to the wall of the pipe and the velocity of solution flow increases in parabolic fashion to a maximum value in the centre of the tube (Fig. 2–4a). Thus, the rate of volume flow calculated from the equation is actually a mean rate averaged over the whole cross sectional area. The mean rate of linear flow of solution in this system,

$$\frac{dL}{dt} = \frac{\Delta P r^2}{8\eta L}$$

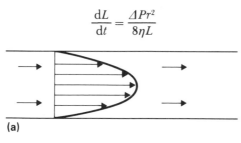

(a)

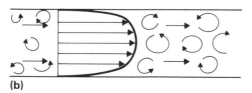

(b)

Fig. 2–4   (a) Laminar flow: the velocity is distributed parabolically across the diameter of the pipe and the fluid moves in layers. (b) Turbulent flow: produces a more uniform distribution of velocity than laminar flow. When the flow is turbulent the fluid moves in random highly irregular paths so that there is exchange of momentum between different parts of the liquid.

As the rate of water movement increases, a transition from laminar to turbulent flow (Fig. 2–4b) occurs and the Poiseuille equation can no longer be applied.

As water moves from A into B (Fig. 2–3), ΔP decreases until it becomes zero and flow stops. Further transfer of water from A to B could be brought about either by applying a positive pressure to the water in A or by exerting a negative pressure (suction) to the liquid in B. In either case the hydrostatic pressure of the water in A would be increased above that in B and water would flow along the pressure gradient, until either all the water was transferred from A to B or the hydrostatic pressure gradient was balanced by the weight of the water accumulating in B.

2.4.2   Diffusion

In contrast to mass flow, diffusion involves the random spontaneous movement of individual particles. Net diffusion of both water and dissolved substances occurs when there is a difference in energy content (chemical potential) between a component in one part of a system and another. A substance which is more concentrated in one place usually has a higher chemical potential, and diffuses towards a region where the concentration (or 'activity') is lower. Thus, when a lump of sugar is dissolved in water there is net diffusion of sugar molecules away from the lump, where they are more concentrated, into parts of the solution which are more dilute and, at the same time, water molecules diffuse from the water, where they are more concentrated, into the lump of sugar. An equilibrium is established when both water and solute molecules are distributed equally throughout the solution.

The net rate of diffusion of a substance can be calculated from Fick's law:

$$\frac{dn}{dt} = -Da\frac{dc}{dx}$$

where dn is the number of molecules which pass in time dt across an area a, and dc is the difference in chemical potential over a distance dx. D is the diffusion coefficient which varies for different substances and it is affected to some extent by temperature and concentration. The negative sign is a convention to indicate that movement is from the higher to the lower concentration.

2.4.3   Chemical potential

Absolute values for the chemical potential of water in a system cannot be obtained very easily but relative values of chemical potential can be determined at any point because:

$$\mu_w - \mu_w^0 = RT\ln(e/e^0)$$

where μ_w is the absolute chemical potential of water at any point in the system; μ_w^0, the absolute chemical potential of pure water at atmospheric pressure and the temperature of the system; R, the molar gas constant (8.31 J K^{-1} mol $^{-1}$); ln, natural logarithm; e, the equilibrium vapour pressure of water in the system, at temperature T; and e^0 the equilibrium vapour pressure of pure water at the same temperature and one atmosphere pressure.

The unit of RT ln (e/e^0) is J mol^{-1}, that is, energy per quantity of substance. It is usually more convenient however in discussions of plant-water relations to use units of pressure (Pascals, bars or atmospheres see Table 4, p. 14), that is energy per unit volume. Energy per mole can be converted to energy per unit volume by dividing by the partial molar volume, $\bar{V}$, that is the volume occupied by one mole of the substance.

2.4.4   Water potential

The difference in chemical potential of water at any point in a system and that of pure water at the same temperature and atmospheric pressure (10^2 kPa) is referred to as the *water potential*, ψ. The water potential of pure water at 25°C and 10^2 kPa pressure is set arbitrarily at zero (cf. temperature scales). Water potential is increased by mechanical pressure or by an increase in temperature; it is lowered by the presence of solutes or by a matrix, such as colloidal particles or charged surfaces; and can be increased or decreased by electro-osmotic effects (see below). Thus water potential may have either a positive or a negative value. In plant systems it is usually negative because the influence of solutes and matrix outweigh other effects. For this reason some plant physiologists prefer the phrase 'depression of water potential' ($\Delta\psi$) which avoids the use of the negative sign, but this can lead to confusion when elevation of water potential has also to be considered (cf. 'diffusion pressure deficit', see p. 31).

Water diffuses from a region of higher to one of lower water potential (cf. transfer of heat from a higher to a lower temperature). The more negative the water potential in a system relative to that outside, the greater the tendency for water to diffuse into the system in accordance with Fick's Law.

Diffusion in liquids and solids, unlike diffusion in gases is a discontinuous process in which at one time a molecule is moving rapidly from one point to another in the system and at another is merely vibrating or rotating around a mean position. The molecule is restrained by forces of attraction between it and surrounding molecules which act as a potential energy barrier. When it acquires sufficient kinetic energy (activation energy) to overcome the barrier a molecule becomes free to diffuse until it loses its kinetic energy by molecular collisions, or in some other way.

When the potential energy barrier is comparatively low, as in the diffusion of small molecules or ions in water at physiological temperatures, the activation energy of diffusion is low and the temperature coefficient (Q_{10}, see Glossary) of the process is near to unity (often $\simeq 1.2–1.3$). On the other hand, when the potential energy barrier is high, as for example for diffusion through a viscous fluid or across a lipid membrane, the activation energy of diffusion is higher and the process has a correspondingly high Q_{10} (often 2–3).

The permeability of a membrane, that is the ease or difficulty with which a particular substance such as water or a dissolved solute diffuses across it, may be represented by a permeability coefficient K (cf. diffusion coefficient, D). K for water, termed 'hydraulic conductivity', and usually represented by L_p, is defined as the distance moved by molecules in unit time for a given gradient of water potential. That is:

$$\frac{\mathrm{d}v}{\mathrm{d}t} = -L_p a \mathrm{d}\psi$$

where $\mathrm{d}v$ is the volume of water passing in time, $\mathrm{d}t$, across area, a, and $\mathrm{d}\psi$ is the difference in water potential across the membrane. The units of L_p are $\mathrm{m.Pa^{-1}\,s^{-1}}$.

A biological membrane is believed to consist basically of a bimolecular layer of oriented phospholipid molecules coated on each surface with a layer of protein (Fig. 2–5). It is thought that water permeates such a membrane through minute pores lined with protein, which are too small to allow most dissolved substances to pass through. This is possible despite the association of water molecules with one another (as described above) because they readily become oriented into files of sufficiently small

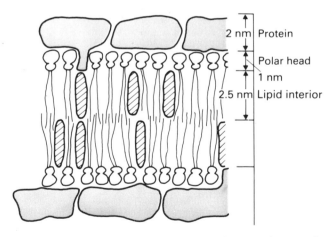

Fig. 2–5   Tentative model of a biological membrane. The protein on the membrane surfaces is largely in association with the polar heads of phospholipids, but in one instance (top left) it is shown intruding into the hydrophobic lipid interior. The hatched, rod-shaped areas represent lipid molecules such as cholesterol. (From CLARKSON, 1974.)

dimensions. The resistance of membranes to diffusion of water is thus many times lower than that of most solutes.

Special mechanisms requiring metabolic energy exist in biological membranes to transport organic molecules and ions into cells where they are retained by the low permeability of the membranes (see SUTCLIFFE and BAKER, 1974). There have been suggestions from time to time that active transport of water occurs in plants, but this possibility has now been largely discounted (see § 3.11 below).

2.4.5   Osmosis

When an aqueous solution, for example of sucrose, is separated from pure water by a membrane which is more permeable to water than it is to the solute (a so-called semi-permeable membrane, S.P.M.) more water molecules diffuse in a given time from the pure solvent into the solution than in the reverse direction in response to the existing gradient of water potential. Such movement, known as osmosis can be demonstrated in an apparatus such as that shown in Fig. 2–6. Although it is generally applied only to systems in which there is differential movement of water, the term 'osmosis' may strictly be applied to the diffusion of any substance across a differentially-permeable membrane in response to a gradient of chemical potential.

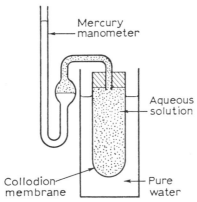

Fig. 2–6   A simple osmometer. For explanation, see text.

The rate of movement of water across the membrane of an osmometer gradually falls, partly because of dilution of the solution inside, and partly because of increased hydrostatic pressure as the column of water rises. Both factors contribute to an increase in the water potential of the inner solution and a consequent decrease in the water potential gradient. Equilibrium is established when the hydrostatic pressure developed balances the effect of the presence of solutes so that the difference in water potential inside and outside the osmometer disappears.

The amount of the excess pressure which must be applied to the solution in an osmometer, with pure water outside a membrane which is impermeable to the solute, is termed the 'osmotic pressure' of the solution (π) and is usually quoted as a positive value. Since no actual pressure is developed unless the solution is placed in an osmometer it is considered preferable nowadays to use the term 'osmotic potential' instead of osmotic pressure when referring to the property of solutions and to give it a negative sign (see Table 6). *Osmotic potential is thus equal to the water potential of a solution when there is no matric potential (see below) and the system is at atmosphere pressure. It is given the symbol ψ_π, and is sometimes referred to as 'solute potential' and designated ψ_s* :

$$\psi_\pi = \psi_s = -\pi$$

The great German plant physiologist, PFEFFER (1877) demonstrated that the osmotic pressure developed by dilute aqueous solutions of sucrose is directly proportional to the concentration of solute and the absolute temperature. His observations led the Dutch chemist, van't Hoff to formulate the kinetic theory of dilute solutions and establish the applicability of the gas-law equation $PV = RT$.

Table 6   Osmotic potential (kPa) of solutions of given molal* and molar† concentration at 20°C.

Conc.	Sucrose		KCl	NaCl
	Molal	*Molar*	*Molar*	*Molar*
0.1	− 260	− 270	− 470	− 440
0.2	− 520	− 540	− 890	− 850
0.3	− 770	− 820	−1280	−1260
0.4	−1020	−1120	−1690	−1680
0.5	−1300	−1450	−2080	−2120
0.6	−1560	−1800	−2440	−2600
0.7	−1830	−2170	−2870	−3010
0.8	−2110	−2580	−3260	−3470
0.9	−2400	−3010	−3640	−3910
1.0	−2690	−3510	−3970	−4380

* A molal solution is 1 mole in 1000 g of water.
† A molar solution is 1 mole in 1 litre of solution.

Thus

$$\pi = \frac{n}{V} \cdot RT$$

and

$$\psi_\pi = -\frac{n}{V} \cdot RT$$

where n is the number of moles of solute in V litres of solution, R is the gas constant and T, the absolute temperature.

The osmotic pressure exerted by a solution in an osmometer at extreme dilution is thus equal to the pressure that the solute molecules would exert if they were in gaseous form occupying a volume equal to that of the solution. This led to the idea, by analogy with the behaviour of molecules in a gas, that osmotic pressure is produced by bombardment of solute molecules against the semi-permeable membrane. This view fails to take account of the fact that the component of the solution which actually moves is the solvent and modern interpretations of osmotic pressure (or potential) invoke the influence of solute in effectively diluting the water and hence lowering its potential. Measurements of the rates of movement of water in osmotic systems now suggest that part of the flow may be by pressure-induced bulk flow rather than by diffusion. If it is assumed that the pores of the membrane are filled with pure water (Fig. 2–7), water molecules close to the solution will tend to diffuse out of the pore causing the density at point B to be lower than at A. This will result in a pressure gradient between A and B which may be the driving force for osmotic bulk flow.

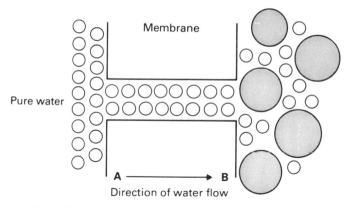

Fig. 2–7 Flow of water through a pore in a semi-permeable membrane. Water molecules (small circles) fill the pore and a sharp discontinuity exists between water and solution at B. Diffusion of water into the solution causes development of a pressure gradient in the pore which causes bulk flow of water from A to B (see text).

On the basis of the van's Hoff equation a molar solution of a non-electrolyte such as sucrose should have an osmotic potential of -2270 kPA (-22.7 bars$\simeq-22.4$ atm) at NTP. In fact, experimentally determined values are appreciably lower (that is more negative) than the theoretical (Table 6). This is attributable to various causes, including association between solvent molecules, hydration of the solute molecules, and to the fact that 1 litre of solution contains less than 1000 g of water because of the volume occupied by solute (cf. molal solution, Table 6).

The osmotic potential of an aqueous solution of an electrolyte is more negative than that of a non-electrolyte at equimolar concentration (Table 6). This is because an electrolyte dissociates into ions and osmotic potential is proportional to the number of solute particles, whether molecules or ions, in the solution. It was from the apparently anomalous values of osmotic potential observed with salt solutions by Pfeffer that Arrhenius was led to propose the ionic theory of solutions.

If two aqueous solutions have the same osmotic potential they are said to be iso-osmotic irrespective of the solute and its concentration. A solution which has a higher (less negative) osmotic potential (i.e. lower osmotic pressure) is said to be hypo-osmotic in comparison with one of lower osmotic potential, which would be termed hyper-osmotic with respect to the other. The synonymous terms 'isotonic', 'hypotonic' and 'hypertonic' are sometimes used by biologists, especially by animal physiologists.

2.4.6   Measurement of osmotic potential

The osmotic potential of a solution can be measured by means of an osmometer as described above. Alternatively, it can be determined by comparison with solutions of known osmotic potential using Barger's method. Small drops of the solution to be examined and of solutions of a range of known osmotic potentials are placed alternately in a capillary tube of about 1 mm bore. If the inner surface of the tube is coated first with a layer of liquid silicone the drops remain discrete and their length can be measured accurately with the aid of a travelling microscope. Water diffuses across an air gap from a hypo-osmotic to a hyper-osmotic solution and when a pair is found in which the drops do not change in size over a period of time, it is concluded that these solutions have the same osmotic potential.

A more accurate method of determining the osmotic potential of a solution is by measurement of the depression of the freezing point (cryoscopic method) which can be done accurately on a small quantity of solution with the aid of a thermocouple. The depression of the freezing point ΔT in °C is related to osmotic potential, ψ_π, in kPa thus:

$$\psi_\pi = -1222\,\Delta T$$

This formula gives the value at 0°C and to calculate osmotic potential of a solution at any given temperature, X°C, it must be multiplied by $(273 + X)/273$.

Osmotic potential can also be measured using a thermocouple psychrometer by means of which the temperature of a drop of solution from which water is evaporating under standard conditions can be determined. The apparatus is calibrated using solutions of known osmotic potential. Alternatively, the vapour pressure of the air in an enclosed chamber above the solution can be measured at equilibrium by making use of the Peltier effect (SPANNER, 1951).

2.4.7   Matric potential

If a substance which is in contact with an aqueous solution attracts water molecules it will lower the water potential. To this component the term matric potential, ψ_m or ψ_τ, is applied. As has been indicated above (p. 16) dissolved molecules and ions attract water to some extent and so contribute to ψ_m as well as to ψ_π. Large molecules, such as those of proteins, which because of their low solubility usually make a relatively small contribution to ψ_π, may nevertheless greatly affect ψ_m. Matric potential is the cause of the swelling of such substances as gelatine and cellulose in water, and is largely responsible for the initial swelling of soaked seeds. A considerable pressure may be developed by a swelling matrix if it is placed in a confined space. It has been estimated that air-dry pea seeds ground into a fine powder may cause the development of pressures in excess of 10^6Pa ($\psi_m = -1000$ kPa). Dry soils absorb and retain water mainly through the operation of matric forces (see Chapter 6).

Water diffuses into an imbibing matrix along a gradient of water potential caused by a lowering of the chemical potential of the water at the surface of the matrix. As more water is absorbed, ψ_m increases (i.e. becomes less negative) and an equilibrium is attained when the potentials of water in the matrix and bathing solution are the same. To extract water from such a system it is necessary to lower the potential of water in the solution, e.g. by addition of a solute. The relationship between ψ_π of the solution and the amount of water withdrawn from the matrix is however not a simple one, because the first molecules of water attracted to a matrix are held by much greater forces than those adsorbed later. Therefore, it is possible to remove an appreciable amount of water from a water-saturated matrix by decreasing the osmotic potential of the external solution by a few Pa, but as the concentration of solution increases, progressively larger changes of osmotic potential are necessary to achieve the same effect.

It is extremely difficult to remove all traces of water from a biological material or from soil because of the large increase in matric potential as water content is reduced (see Fig. 6–8).

2.4.8   Electro-osmosis

When an electrical potential gradient is established in an aqueous solution containing charged particles there is a migration of the particles through the solvent to the anode (+) or cathode (−) according to their charge. This process is called electrophoresis and is made use of, for example, in the separation of individual proteins from solutions. If, on the other hand, the charged particles are fixed, e.g. on the surface of a

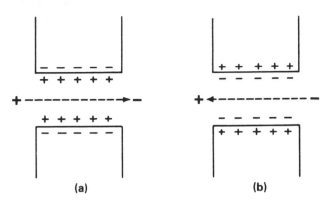

Fig. 2–8   Electro-osmosis: the arrows indicate the direction of flow of water
when the pores of the membrane are charged; (a) –vely; and (b)+ vely.

membrane (see Fig. 2–8), then an electrical potential gradient causes
movement of solvent molecules. Such movement is known as electro-
osmosis. Negative charges in the wall of a pore induce positive charges in
the surface layers of water molecules within the pore and the charged
water then moves in the direction of the negative pole in response to an
electro-chemical potential gradient (Fig. 2–8a). Conversely, positively-
charged pore surfaces induce negative charges in the water and cause
movement in the reverse direction (Fig. 2–8b). Electro-osmotic water
movement occurs by bulk flow, not by diffusion and may carry dissolved
substances along with it. Electro-osmosis has been invoked to account for
some water movement in plants, e.g. in the phloem (see below).

3 Water Relations of Cells and Tissues

3.1 The vacuolated plant cell

Much of the tissue of a plant is composed of highly vacuolated cells to which the term parenchyma ('packing-tissue') is applied. The structure of a typical parenchyma cell from a non-green part of a plant is represented diagrammatically in Fig. 3–1. The cell wall is a relatively rigid structure, but it also has a certain degree of elasticity. The walls of some vacuolated cells (e.g. xylem parenchyma) are impregnated with lignin, and are much more rigid than say those of collenchyma where the walls contain a high percentage of cellulose and pectic compounds. Except when it has a large

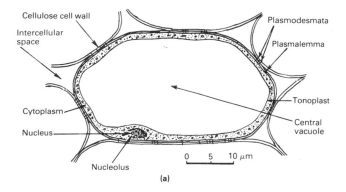

(a)

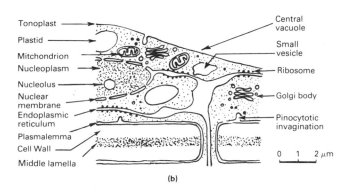

(b)

Fig. 3–1 Structure of a vacuolated plant cell. (a) Low magnification; (b) ultra-microscopic structure.

amount of lipids, as for example in cork cells, a cell wall is highly permeable to both water and dissolved substances, i.e. it has a high hydraulic conductivity (see p. 47). The space between solid material in the wall is infiltrated by the solution in which the cells are bathed, hence it is sometimes referred to as 'free space'.

Characteristically, the cytoplasm forms a thin layer lining the inner surface of the cell wall; and it is bounded on the outside by a lipoprotein membrane – the plasma membrane or plasmalemma. The plasmalemma is much thinner than the cell wall (only some 8–10 nm) but because of its structure it is much less permeable to water, and particularly to solutes (see Fig. 2–5). The structure of the underlying cytoplasm is complex as is shown in Fig. 3–1b. There is an internal system of membranes, the endoplasmic reticulum, which effectively divides the cytoplasm into two phases – one of which contains an aqueous solution of inorganic and organic solutes, and the other a variety of membrane-bound organelles, including nucleus, mitochondria, plastids, Golgi bodies and small isolated vesicles. The cytoplasm of one cell is continuous with that of its neighbours through protoplasmic connections or plasmodesmata and the whole system of interconnected cytoplasts is called a symplast (or symplasm).

Most of the volume of a parenchyma cell is taken up by one or more large vacuoles which are filled with an aqueous solution of inorganic and organic substances. The concentration of these substances is such that the vacuolar sap commonly has an osmotic potential in the range of − 500 to −3000 kPa (−5 to −30 bars) and in exceptional cases osmotic potentials as low as − 20 000 kPa have been reported in halophytes. The vacuole acts as a depository for substances which are not immediately required by the plant and for unwanted products of metabolism, and it has an important role in the maintenance of cell turgidity (see below, p. 31). It is bounded by a membrane, called the tonoplast, which resembles the plasmalemma in structure and is presumed to regulate the movement of materials between cytoplasm and vacuole. Vacuoles are formed during cell development by coalescence of small cytoplasmic vesicles which are present in embryonic (meristematic) cells.

3.2   Water relations of a vacuolated cell

The cytoplasm of a vacuolated cell such as that represented in Fig. 3–1a behaves as a semi-permeable membrane separating the central vacuole from the external solution bathing the cell wall. Because the volume of cytoplasm is relatively small compared with that of the vacuole it is customary to treat the water relations of a vacuolated cell as if the cytoplasm was a simple membrane of negligible thickness. This is obviously an over-simplification as in many vacuolated cells cytoplasmic volume is an appreciable fraction (10% or more) of total cell volume, and furthermore it does not remain constant under different conditions. As vacuolar volume alters with changes in the water potential of the medium so presumably does cytoplasmic volume also. When a cell reaches equilibrium under a particular set of conditions the water potentials of vacuole and of the various compartments within the cytoplasm will be equal and there will be no further movement of water from one place to another other than the small amount induced by metabolic processes in which water is consumed or produced.

The idea that a vacuolated plant cell behaves as an osmometer emerged during the later part of the nineteenth century, mainly through the work of W. Pfeffer, and a Dutch botanist, Hugo de Vries. At first, only the difference in osmotic potential (then called osmotic pressure) between the vacuolar sap and bathing solution was considered to be important, but it soon became clear that the mechanical pressure exerted by the stretched wall of a turgid cell must also be taken into account. In accordance with Newton's third law of motion, this wall pressure causes an equal and oppositely-directed counter pressure which is called turgor pressure. These two terms are often confused and it is important to appreciate that although equal in magnitude they are exerted in opposite directions. Thus, although wall pressure is exerted inwards, it causes, through turgor pressure, an increase in cell turgidity (cf. a pneumatic tyre).

The force responsible for water entering the vacuole (called by early German workers e.g. A. Ursprung and G. Blum, 'saugkraft' or 'suction force') was thus seen to be the result of two separate forces, namely the difference in osmotic potential between vacuolar sap and external solution, which tends to cause water to enter the cell, and the mechanical pressure exerted by the wall, which tends to squeeze water out.

The use of the terms suction force and suction pressure were soon criticized on the grounds that suction is not involved and after several alternative names had been rejected the American botanist, B. S. MEYER (1945), introduced the term 'diffusion pressure deficit' (DPD) to replace them. The DPD of water in a solution (e.g. vacuolar sap) was defined as the amount by which the 'diffusion pressure' of water in it is less than that of pure water at the same temperature and pressure. Water would move by diffusion from a solution of lower to one of higher DPD, and in the case of a cell would stop when the DPD of the vacuolar sap became the same as that of the external solution. This terminology was widely used for a time in the United States and was gradually being accepted elsewhere until the advantages of using the concept of *water potential* were pointed out by KRAMER, KNIPLING and MILLER (1966). Since then the water potential terminology has become recognized as superior and it is used in this booklet and in most modern text books of plant physiology.

The advantages of the water potential terminology are:

(i) It is based on broad thermodynamic concepts and thus plant water-relations can be described in terms that are readily understood by a physical chemist as well as by biologists.

(ii) Because these concepts can be applied to the physical environment as well as to living organisms it enables soil scientists, plant physiologists, and meteorologists to use a common language, and a unified description of water movement from soil through a plant into the air becomes possible (see Chapter 6).

(iii) The older terminologies were applicable only to vacuolated cells and the phenomenon of imbibition which is important, e.g. in the uptake of water by germinating seeds, or retention by dry soil, had to be discussed as a separate process. The water potential terminology enables imbibition to be considered within the same basic concepts as osmosis.

It is hoped that the attractiveness of the water potential terminology will become clear in the descriptions of cell, tissue and whole plant water relations which follows. A list of the terms used and recommended symbols is given in Table 7.

Table 7   Terms and symbols used in the description of plant water relations.

Term	Recommended Symbol	Alternative symbol
Water potential	ψ (psi)	$-DPD$ (obsolete)
Water potential of:		
cytoplasm	ψ_c	
vacuolar sap	ψ_v	
xylem sap	ψ_x	
external solution	ψ_e	
cell	ψ_{cell}	
soil	ψ_{soil}	
air	ψ_{air}	
Osmotic potential	ψ_π	ψ_s ; $-\pi$; $-OP$ (obsolete)
(solute potential)		
osmotic pressure	π	$-\psi_\pi$; OP (obsolete)
matric potential	ψ_m	ψ_τ ; τ (tau)
pressure potential	ψ_p	ψ_w; P; WP (obsolete)
(wall pressure)		
cytoplasmic pressure	ψ_{cp}	
turgor pressure	$\psi_t (=\psi_p)$	P; TP (obsolete)
hydraulic conductivity	L_p	
elastic coefficient	ϵ (epsilon)	
(Young's modulus)		

The water potential of the sap, ψ_v, of a vacuolated cell under isothermal conditions is determined by the concentration of solutes in the vacuole, the amount of water-binding substances, and the pressure exerted by the cell wall in accordance with the equation:

$$\psi_v = \psi_\pi + \psi_m + \psi_p$$

where ψ_π, ψ_m and ψ_p are the contributions made by solutes, matrix and pressure respectively.

ψ_π and ψ_m are negative quantities, while ψ_p is generally positive. Water is taken up by the cell vacuole as long as ψ_v is more negative than the potential of water in the bathing solution (ψ_e). Uptake of water dilutes the vacuolar sap and raises ψ_π (i.e. it becomes less negative, and at the same time, because the cell swells, ψ_p also increases (i.e. it becomes more positive). Thus the value of ψ_v increases until it becomes equal to ψ_e at which point uptake of water stops. If the bathing solution is pure water ($\psi_e = 0$), then at equilibrium, $\psi_v = 0$ and the cell is then fully turgid. Under such conditions

$$-\psi_p = \psi_\pi + \psi_m$$

and both ψ_p and ψ_t (turgor pressure) are maximal.

On the other hand, if the external solution contains solutes (i.e. $\psi_e < 0$) equilibrium is established at less than maximum cell volume, i.e. before the cell reaches full turgidity. At this point

$$-\psi_p = \psi_\pi + \psi_m - \psi_e$$

A solution in which a cell remains exactly the same volume as *in vivo* is said to be *isotonic* with the cell. A *hypertonic* solution is one in which a cell shrinks and a *hypotonic* solution is one in which it swells.

Figure 3–2 illustrates diagrammatically the changes which occurred in ψ_v, ψ_π and ψ_p when a vacuolated cell of *Nitella* sp. was allowed to swell or shrink by being placed in sucrose solutions of various osmotic potentials. Estimates of cell volume were obtained by microscopic observation; ψ_π was calculated at each point from the estimates of cell volume assuming that the amount of solute in the vacuole remained the same and the volume of the cytoplasm was negligible; ψ_p was calculated by difference assuming ψ_m to be negligible.

In the particular cell examined the cell volume at turgidity was 4% larger than in the solution in which ψ_p was just reduced to zero (the point of incipient plasmolysis). The extent of the volume change observed in different cells depends on the degree of elasticity of the wall, that is on their elastic coefficient, ϵ. In some lignified parenchyma cells the change in volume between full turgidity and incipient plasmolysis is only a fraction of 1%, while in cells with very extensible cell walls, e.g. guard cells (see Chapter 4), a change in volume of up to 50% may occur. It is worth noting that the curve for ψ_p is concave to the horizontal axis; this means that as the cell enlarges a given change in cell volume produces a progressively larger effect on ψ_p until the wall is fully extended, at which time uptake of water stops. Young cells generally have more extensible walls than mature cells and when they are growing, ψ_p is maintained at a low value so that uptake of water continues over a prolonged period (see below).

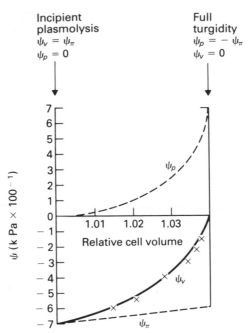

Fig. 3–2 Relationships between ψ_v, ψ_π, ψ_p and cell volume in a vacuolated plant cell of *Nitella* sp. Note that ψ_v and ψ_π becomes less negative and ψ_p more positive as the cell increases in volume. For further explanation, see text. (Data of TAMIYA, 1938.)

3.3 Plasmolysis

If a vacuolated cell is placed in a solution of such low water potential that equilibrium is not attained by the time ψ_p falls to zero, water will continue to be withdrawn from the vacuole because a gradient of water potential still exists. At first the cell wall may cave in slightly through adhesion to the cytoplasm with development of a small negative ψ_p, but, if, as is usual, the solute is able to diffuse through the cell wall, the wall and protoplast begin to part company, (incipient plasmolysis). The wall returns to its undistorted condition ($\psi_p = 0$) and the protoplasm continues to contract with the vacuole causing the cells to become plasmolysed (Fig. 3–3). The space between the cell wall and plasmalemma (called the intra-mural space) is filled with the external solution to which the vacuole continues to lose water until ψ_v and ψ_e are equal. At this point, as ψ_p is zero, ψ_π of the cell sap is equal to ψ_e, assuming that ψ_m and the hydrostatic pressure resulting from the enclosing cytoplasm (cytoplasmic pressure, ψ_{cp}) are negligible. The latter has never been measured accurately in plant cells, but red blood cells are said to have a cytoplasmic

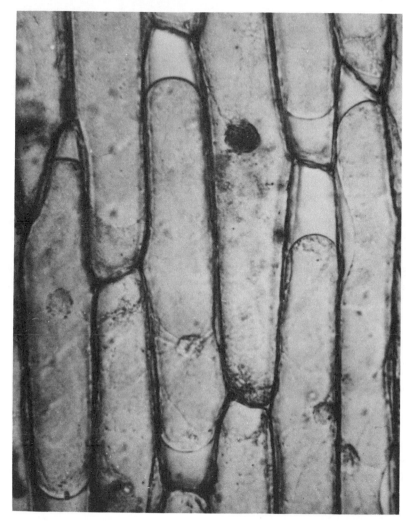

Fig. 3–3   Onion bulb scale epidermal cells mounted in 0·5 M sucrose solution. Note that some, but not all, of the cells are plasmolysed.

pressure equivalent to about 300 Pa and that of plasmolysed plant cells may be of the same order.

On plasmolysis the cytoplasm may assume one of several forms, as shown in Fig. 3–4. Convex plasmolysis (Fig. 3–4a) generally occurs in mature cells and seems to be associated with relatively low cytoplasmic viscosity and easy separation of wall from cytoplasm. In concave plasmolysis (Fig. 3–4b), in which the cytoplasm may assume a variety of

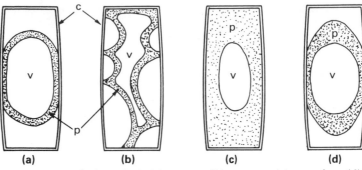

Fig. 3-4   Types of plasmolysis (a) convex, (b) concave, (c) tonoplast, (d) cap.
c = cell wall; p = protoplasm; v = vacuole.

irregular shapes, the plasmalemma adheres to the wall at various points, probably in the region of plasmodesmata. Calcium salts often cause concave plasmolysis while potassium salts usually induce convex plasmolysis. Concave plasmolysis often alters to the convex form when plasmolysis is prolonged. In plasmolysed cells many very fine strands of cytoplasm (strands of Hecht) can sometimes be seen running between the wall and cytoplasmic surface.

The fact that the cytoplasm separates from the cell wall on plasmolysis shows that while the wall allows both water and dissolved substances to pass through it, the layer of cytoplasm behaves as a semi-permeable membrane. Semi-permeability properties may be associated with the plasmalemma or tonoplast or with both. If only the plasmalemma was involved the volume of the cytoplasm would decrease on plasmolysis to the same extent as that of the vacuole. On the other hand, if the tonoplast was the sole functional membrane only the vacuole would contract and the volume of cytoplasm would increase correspondingly. This appears to occur in tonoplast plasmolysis (Fig. 3-4c) which can be induced by treatment of cells with certain solutions, e.g. potassium thiocyanate. This treatment apparently destroys the semi-permeability properties of the plasmalemma and appears to show that the tonoplast is also semi-permeable. Unlike convex and concave plasmolysis tonoplast plasmolysis cannot be reversed, presumably because the cytoplasm has been irreversibly injured. Cap plasmolysis is an intermediate condition in which the cytoplasm swells at the ends of the cell (Fig. 3-4d). This observation also is best explained by postulating that both the plasmalemma and tonoplast are semi-permeable. Some plasmolysed cells can remain alive for an indefinite period and if deplasmolysed slowly they may return to normal without apparent injury. When kept in the plasmolysing solution for a long time, they often begin to deplasmolyse because solutes accumulate from the medium and this lowers ψ_π and ψ_v. Such recovery illustrates a feature of the cytoplasmic layer which distinguishes it from a non-living semi-permeable membrane, namely its ability to transport solutes actively. Although cytoplasm has a high resistance to passive penetration of many solutes, ions and some organic molecules are transferred across it unidirectionally even against an existing electro-chemical gradient, albeit at a slow rate relative to the rate of movement of water (see SUTCLIFFE and BAKER, 1974).

Solutions containing solutes which can diffuse passively into cell vacuoles or which are accumulated actively, are not as effective plasmolysing agents as solutions containing solutes which do not penetrate. It is possible to make an estimate of the rate of passive penetration of solutes into cells by comparing the degree of plasmolysis induced by iso-osmotic solutions containing non-penetrating and penetrating solutes (see reflection coefficient, p. 46). There are some solutes, e.g. various alcohols which enter cells so quickly that plasmolysis does not occur at all. There are others, e.g. polyethyleneglycol (PEG) in which the molecules are too large to pass through the cell wall. Concentrated solutions of such solutes cannot induce plasmolysis because the cell wall is semi-permeable to them; instead they cause the cell wall to collapse if water continues to be withdrawn after ψ_p falls to zero. This phenomenon, which is called *cytorrhysis*, occurs sometimes when cells are placed in strong solutions of slowly-penetrating solutes such as sucrose, presumably because the cytoplasm adheres so strongly to the cell wall that it does not separate from the wall but pulls it in as the protoplast contracts. Cytorrhysis also takes place when the supply of water to a tissue, e.g. a leaf, is cut off and it is allowed to dry out in air. The air cannot penetrate between the wall and cytoplasm to allow plasmolysis but the water potential gradient between the tissue and air is sufficient to cause the cells to collapse when sufficient water has evaporated.

Plasmolysis is a very rare occurrence in nature because cells are not often bathed in solutions of lower ψ_π than that of the vacuolar sap. The cells of plant roots adapted to grow in solutions of low osmotic potential (high osmotic pressure), e.g. sea-water, have a correspondingly more highly concentrated vacuolar sap. However, if there is a rapid decrease in ψ_π of the external solution, e.g. as a result of evaporation of water from salt pans on hots days, the cells might not have time to adjust and become plasmolysed temporarily.

3.4 Water relations of parenchyma

Individual cells in a tissue are subjected to pressures or tensions imposed on them by surrounding cells, and for this reason the water potential of a cell after it has been isolated is usually significantly different from that of the same cell in the intact organism. If a given cell is subjected to compression by those surrounding it, its ψ_p will be effectively increased and ψ_v increased. Conversely, if the cells are being stretched by their adherence to surrounding tissues, the pressure potential may be reduced and in extreme cases ψ_p can become negative.

Tissue tensions cause curvature at the cut end of hollow stems and inflorescence stalks such as those of the dandelion (*Taraxacum officinale*) when placed in water. The pressure potential of the inner cells of the tissue is reduced by release of tension and ψ_v falls causing the cells to take up water from the medium and swell to a greater extent than those nearer the surface which are prevented from expanding by a rigid cuticle.

All the cells in a tissue at equilibrium have the same water potential because those which have initially a more negative ψ_v withdraw water from surrounding cells in which ψ_v is higher. However, it must be emphasized that the osmotic potential of the sap in individual cells may be widely different. Cells with a low osmotic potential will have a correspondingly higher turgor pressure at equilibrium than those in which the osmotic potential is high (see Table 8).

Table 8 Approximate values of ψ_π and ψ_p (in kPa) for three cells, A, B, and C, with different values of ψ_π, when at equilibrium in water and in a solution having an osmotic potential of −1000 kPa.

The values of ψ_π and ψ_p for the cells in the later solution are calculated from the estimated volumes of vacuole, V, in the cells at different degrees of turgidity. V is expressed as a percentage of its value when the cells are in pure water. The gas-law relationship is assumed to hold and matric potential to be negligible.

ψ_e (kPa)		Cells		
		A	B	C
0	ψ_π	−500	−1000	−1500
	ψ_p	500	1000	1500
	V	100	100	100
−1000	ψ_π	−1000	−1180	−1690
	ψ_p	0	180	690
	V	50*	85	89

* Cell plasmolysed.

3.5   Measurement of water potential

The water potential of a vacuolated cell is largely determined by ψ_v, the water potential of the vacuolar sap. Water is taken up from a solution of higher water potential and released to one of lower water potential than the sap. Most methods of estimating the water potential of a cell or tissue involve a determination of the water potential of the medium in which the cell or cells neither take up nor lose water. It is difficult, if not impossible to determine the water potential of cells in an intact multicellular plant, and since the potential begins to change immediately on excision, e.g. by release of tissue tensions, evaporation, etc., measurements made on isolated tissue are no more than approximate estimates of the values *in situ*. It is important that measurements should be made as quickly as possible after excision.

The following methods have been used successfully to measure water potential of cells, tissues and organs.

3.5.1   Volume methods

A method based on measurement under the microscope of changes in the linear dimension of cells placed in solutions of different osmotic potential was used in the early nineteen hundreds by Ursprung and Blum to determine the 'suction force' of individual cells. The method has been modified to enable the mean water potential of a population of cells to be estimated. Strips of homogeneous tissue, say about 2 cm long and 2 mm wide are removed from the plant organ, e.g. a potato tuber, and transferred to a glass slide. The length of each strip is measured as accurately as possible using a millimetre scale and the strips are then placed in a series of solutions of a slowly-penetrating solute such as sucrose or mannitol for about one hour. The strips are then re-measured and the results plotted graphically. The water potential of the solution in which the strips do not change in length is taken as the same as that of the strips (Fig. 3–5).

If the structure of a tissue is not homogeneous such that it is prevented from swelling or contracting on one side, e.g. by the presence of a rigid cuticle or thick-walled cells, the water potential of cells on the other side can be gauged from the degree of curvature which results when pieces of

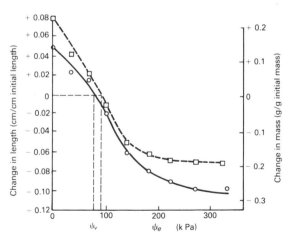

Fig. 3–5   Determination of the water potential of potato tuber tissue by the volume (☐– – –☐) and weighing (o——o) methods. (Data of MEYER and WALLACE, 1941.) For explanation, see text.

tissue are immersed in solutions of different osmotic potential. A solution in which a straight piece of tissue does not curve had a water potential approximately the same as that of the cells under investigation. Segments of pea stem internodes, dandelion inflorescence stalks and dock leaf petioles cut longitudially into quadrants can be used to demonstrate this method.

3.5.2   Gravimetric methods

Thin slices of tissue are weighed quickly on a sensitive balance and placed in a graded series of solutions of known osmotic potential as in section 3.5.1. After equilibration for about one hour the experimental material is removed, dried superficially between filter papers, and weighed again. The solution in which no change in weight occurs is taken to have a water potential corresponding to that of the tissue (Fig. 3–5).

Successful application of this method depends on the rapidity with which the weighings are made and standardization of the drying procedure. Good results can sometimes be obtained using a sensitive spring balance or a weight transducer (see IDLE, 1976) with which it is possible to weigh the tissue quickly. The method tends to give too low an estimate of ψ_v because there is often some displacement of air from intercellular spaces which causes an increase in weight when the tissue is placed in a solution having the same water potential as the vacuolar sap. As in the volume method there is a risk of some solute penetrating into the vacuole during equilibration, thus lowering ψ_π and ψ_v.

Both of these problems are avoided if instead of immersing the tissue in water it is allowed to equilibrate in moist air maintained at various vapour pressures. The quantity of water transferred from tissue to air or vice versa will depend on the magnitude of the difference in water potential between the tissue and air. A problem with this method is that the temperature must be controlled very precisely because the relationship between water potential and vapour pressure varies with temperature.

3.5.3   Chardakov's method

The methods described in sections 3.5.1 and 3.5.2 are designed to measure directly changes in the water content of the tissue when it is placed in solutions of different osmotic potentials. Water transfer between tissue and solution can also be determined by measuring changes in the solution. A simple way to do this is to colour a series of sucrose or mannitol solutions of known osmotic potentials, with a dye such as methylene blue. Pieces of the tissue whose water potential is to be determined are first immersed in unstained aliquots (say 10 cm³) of the osmotica and allowed to equilibrate for about an hour. The tissue is then removed and a drop of the coloured solution of corresponding osmotic potential is added carefully through a pipette below the surface of each solution. If water is absorbed by the tissue during immersion the concentration and hence the density of the solution will increase and so the coloured drop will tend to rise, whereas if water is lost from the tissue causing dilution of the solution the coloured drop will sink. The osmotic potential of the solution in which the coloured solution diffuses out of the drop without tendency to rise or fall is taken to be equal to the water potential of the tissue.

3.5.4   A refractometric method

An alternative method of detecting a change in the water content of a solution in presence of the tissue under investigation is to measure changes in the concentration of a solute such as sucrose by means of a refractometer. STOCKING (1945) devised a procedure for determining the water potential of pith cells of intact *Cucurbita* plants by this method. Sugar solutions are injected into the hollow petiole or stem and at intervals samples are withdrawn for analysis. When no change in refractive index is observed it is concluded that the water potential of the solution is the same as that of cells at the inner surface in contact with it.

3.5.5   Psychrometric method

The water potential of a piece of tissue can be measured in the same way as the osmotic potential of a solution using a thermocouple psychrometer (see p. 26). By measuring the temperature of tissue from which water is evaporating into moist air and comparing it with the temperature of solutions of known osmotic potential under the same conditions, the water potential of the tissue can be calculated. This method is probably the most accurate of all the available methods of measuring water potential. Thermocouple psychrometers have now been designed which are not subject to errors due to temperature fluctuations (cf. section 3.5.2). HOFFMAN and RAWLINGS (1972) have developed such a thermocouple psychrometer for use in the field with which the water potential of intact leaves attached to a plant can be measured with a precision of ± 100 kPa.

3.5.6   Pressure chamber method

In this method a leaf or leafy shoot is placed in a chamber capable of withstanding gas pressures up to 5000 kPa or more with the cut end of the periole or stem protruding through a gas tight seal (Fig. 3–6). An inert gas such as nitrogen is admitted under pressure into the chamber and the pressure increased until liquid just appears at the cut surface. At this point equilibrium is considered to have been established between the leaf cells and xylem sap, and the gas pressure is taken to counteract exactly the water potential of the leaf cells. The osmotic potential of the xylem sap is assumed to be negligible and the hydraulic conductivity (see below) so high that the gradient of water potential within the tissue is negligible.

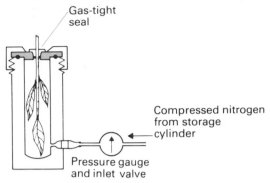

Fig. 3–6 Cross-section through a pressure chamber used to measure water potential of a leafy shoot.

3.6 Measurement of osmotic potential

3.6.1 Methods involving sap extraction

Uncontaminated sap can be extracted from the vacuoles of giant algal coenocytes (e.g. those of *Valonia* spp., which may have a volume of several cm³), by means of a micro-syringe or pipette. Fairly pure vacuolar sap can be obtained from large cells of the fresh-water alga *Nitella* simply by cutting across a filament towards one end of a cell and squeezing the liquid out on to a slide with the aid of a glass rod, like tooth-paste from a tube.

The extraction of uncontaminated sap from cells of higher plants presents much greater difficulty. A sophisticated method of obtaining the sap from sieve tubes in the phloem of an intact plant is to make use of aphids. In order to feed, an aphid inserts its stylets into a vascular bundle and locates a sieve tube. If the stylets are severed then a droplet of phloem sap is exuded through the portion remaining in the plant.

This method does not have general application and it is not easy to make fine enough micropipettes to extract sap from individual cells. The method that is commonly employed for parenchyma cells is to squeeze sap from a tissue under pressure. Care has to be taken to prevent the cells from being ruptured by shearing, and the usual procedure is to arrange piles of leaf discs or tissue slices in a press and squeeze them gradually from above. If the cytoplasmic membranes remain intact and semi-permeable, only water should be squeezed out, so the tissue is frozen and thawed first to make the membranes permeable to solutes. A danger with this technique is that the vacuolar sap may be contaminated with cytoplasmic constituents. The problem is not so serious when the ratio of cytoplasm to vacuolar volume is low as in parenchyma cells.

The osmotic potential of extracted sap can be determined by

cryoscopy, by the use of some kind of osmometer (see Chapter 2, p. 23), or by psychrometry.

3.6.2 The plasmometric method

This method, devised by Hugo de Vries and used extensively by the German physiologist, K. Höfler, is applicable to individual cells. It involves determination of the volume of the cell vacuole initially (V_t) and after plasmolysis (V_p) in a solution of known osmotic potential (ψ_e). The osmotic potential of the original sap (ψ_π) is then calculated from the formula,

$$\psi_\pi = \psi_e \times \frac{V_p}{V_t}$$

on the assumption that at equilibrium the water potential of the sap in the plasmolysed cell is equal to ψ_π, i.e. cytoplasmic pressure and matric potential are negligible and the van't Hoff relationship holds (see p. 24). It is assumed that there is no penetration of solute, i.e. the reflection coefficient is unity.

This method can only be applied with reasonable accuracy to cells which approximate to regular shapes, e.g. spheres, cubes or cylinders, and when the plasmolysed protoplast assumes a regular form so that its vacuolar volume can be calculated from measurement of linear dimensions under the microscope. It is sometimes possible, e.g. in some epidermal cells of onion bulb scales (Fig. 3–3), to treat the cell as a cylinder and the plasmolysed protoplast as a cylinder with hemispherical ends. The volume of the vacuole of the turgid cell (V_t) is then given by the formula: $V_t = \pi r_t{}^2 l_t$, and for the plasmolysed cell: $V_p = \pi r_p{}^2 (l_p - \tfrac{2}{3} r_p)$ where $\pi \simeq 3.14$; l_p and l_t the lengths of the vacuole in the plasmolysed and turgid cell respectively and r_p and r_t the corresponding radii.

In practice it is convenient to plasmolyse a population of cells in the tissue under investigation and then select particular cells for the determination from among those of regular shape which have plasmolysed in a convenient form. With onion epidermal cells which have fairly low elastic coefficients (see below), V_t can be calculated accurately enough by estimating l_t from the position of cell walls in the plasmolysed cells (Fig. 3–3) and r_t can be taken as equal to r_p. When the shape of the vacuole does not change appreciably on plasmolysis, e.g. if the turgid cell has somewhat spherical ends, and only a rough estimate of ψ_π is required there is no need to calculate the volumes at all, and V_p/V_t can be replaced by l_p/l_t which can be expressed in arbitrary units, e.g. micrometer scale divisions.

3.6.3 The method of limiting plasmolysis

This method is based on the assumption that at an incipient plasmolysis, the osmotic potential of the cell sap is equal to that of the external medium, i.e. ψ_p is zero and ψ_m and ψ_c are small enough to be ignored. Since it is difficult to judge accurately the point of incipient plasmolysis in individual cells, the method is useful mainly in estimating the mean osmotic potential of the sap in a population of cells in a homogeneous tissue. Samples of the tissue (thin, 0.5 mm) slices of a storage organ such as red beetroot, and onion epidermal strips can work very well) are placed in solutions of known osmotic potential and allowed to reach equilibrium. This usually takes about 30 minutes. They are then examined with a microscope and the percentage of cells visibly plasmolysed in each solution is recorded. The results can be plotted in the form of a graph (Fig. 3–7) and the osmotic potential corresponding to

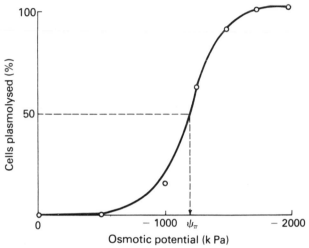

Fig. 3–7   Determination of the mean osmotic potential of vacuolar sap (ψ_π) by the method of limiting plasmolysis. For explanation, see text.

50% plasmolysis is taken to equal the mean value of the vacuolar sap at incipient plasmolysis. In order to convert this value to the osmotic potential of the sap in a turgid cell it is necessary to make a correction for the difference in volume of the vacuole in the two conditions. If ψ_{π_i} is the osmotic potential of the sap at incipient plasmolysis and V_i is the volume of the vacuole at this point, then assuming that the van't Hoff relationship holds:

$$\psi_{\pi_t} = \psi_{\pi_i} \times \frac{V_i}{V_t}$$

when ψ_{π_t} and V_t are respectively the osmotic potential and volume of the sap in the turgid cell. V_i/V_t can be estimated approximately from the ratio of the weights of a piece of tissue when equilibrated in solutions causing incipient plasmolysis and in pure water. The value of V_i/V_t is dependent on the elastic coefficient of the tissue and for some samples of red beetroot tissue is approximately 0.95.

Because of inherent inaccuracies in the methods available it is impossible to determine the exact osmotic potential of vacuolar sap *in situ*. The term 'osmotic value' is sometimes applied to the estimates of osmotic potential that are made especially in cases where matric potential has been ignored. The value of osmotic potential determined by different methods may be expected to differ because of different errors inherent in each method (see below).

3.7   Measurement of matric potential

Two of the methods of estimating osmotic potential described in section 3.6 (sections 3.6.2 and 3.6.3) actually measure $\psi_\pi + \psi_m$ and it has to be assumed that ψ_m is negligible for the methods to be used to estimate ψ_π. On the other hand, ψ_m, however large, does not make a significant contribution to freezing point depression or the psychrometric determination of ψ_π on extracted sap, unless the sap is contaminated with cytoplasmic material. One method of estimating matric potential is to compare the water potential of extracted vacuolar sap with that of the same tissue when it has been frozen and thawed. The water potential measurements can be conveniently done using a thermocouple psychrometer. Because of the loss of permeability of the membranes, ψ_p is reduced to zero in tissue so treated and $\psi_v = \psi_\pi + \psi_m$. As the water potential of the extracted sap is due mainly to ψ_π, any difference in the two determinations can be attributed to ψ_m.

A variation of this method is to use a pressure chamber (p. 41) to measure the water potential of a leaf or leafy shoot that has been frozen and thawed. As the permeability of the membranes has been destroyed the water that remains is held by matric forces alone. The applied pressure which just causes water to be squeezed out is therefore numerically equal (but opposite in sign) to the matric potential.

Matric potentials are commonly −10 kPa or higher for vacuolated tissues and so can safely be disregarded. Much more negative values of ψ_m have been obtained in tissues containing a high proportion of less highly vacuolated cells, e.g. root tips and young leaves. Tissues of xerophytes (p. 9) have highly negative matric potentials especially when they are under water stress. This is because of the large amounts of mucilaginous material associated with cell walls which imbibe water strongly. The lowest matric potentials of all are found in dry seeds where they may go down to -10^5 kPa or less.

3.8   Measurement of pressure potential and the coefficient of elasticity

Until recently pressure potential could only be determined indirectly using the equation:

$$\psi_v = \psi_\pi + \psi_m + \psi_p$$

after measurement of the other three parameters.

One method of measuring ψ_p directly which has been successfully applied to large algal cells (GREEN and STANTON, 1967) is to fuse a micro-capillary tube at one end and insert the open end into the vacuole. It is then possible to calculate the turgor pressure in the cell from the compression of air in the tube. STEUDLE and ZIMMERMANN (1974) have devised a pressure probe by means of which it is possible to measure turgor pressure directly in large cells (Fig. 3–8).

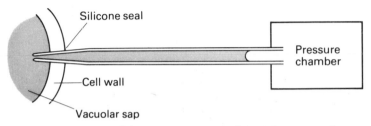

Silicone seal

Pressure
chamber

Cell wall

Vacuolar sap

Fig. 3–8   Measurement of the turgor pressure of a cell by means of a pressure probe. (After STEUDLE and ZIMMERMANN, 1974.)

It is also possible to apply known hydrostatic pressures to the vacuolar contents and from the changes that occur in cell volume (V) when the pressure P is altered the elastic coefficient, can be calculated from the formula:

$$\epsilon = V \frac{\Delta p}{\Delta v}.$$

For a cell with a rigid wall (ϵ small) the volume change for a given change in pressure will be very small, whereas for a cell with very elastic walls (ϵ high) there will be a large change in volume for the same pressure change. Burström (1971b) has described a method of estimating ϵ by measuring the resonance frequency of a piece of tissue. Material such as a length of stem is fastened at one end and caused to vibrate by inserting a piece of steel wire in the free end and placing the tissue in the field of an electro-magnet supplied with alternating currents of different frequencies.

3.9   Measurement of reflection coefficient (σ)

In the discussion so far it has been assumed that cell membranes are permeable to water but totally impermeable to solutes. In fact they are not completely semi-permeable, many solutes can penetrate passively, although many do so only slowly. The reflection coefficient is a measure of the penetration of solutes through a membrane that is freely permeable to water. If completely permeable to solutes σ is zero, and at the other extreme, if the membrane is completely impermeable to solutes the reflection coefficient is one. Thus for differentially permeable membranes σ has values between 0 and 1.0 depending on the specific permeabilities for different solutes and water. Reflection coefficient can be determined from the values of ψ_π measured cryoscopically on extracted sap and plasmolytically after allowance has been made for ψ_m, i.e.

$$\sigma = \frac{\psi_\pi \text{ (cryoscopic)}}{\psi_\pi \text{ (plasmolytic)}}$$

Depending on the rate at which the solute penetrates, ψ_π determined plasmolytically will be lower than ψ_π determined cryoscopically. Values of σ as low as 0.6 to 0.7 have been observed for sucrose in some tissues whereas those for mannitol range from 0.8 to 0.9. If the solute penetrates so quickly that the cells do not plasmolyse ψ_π (plasmolytic) $\longrightarrow \infty$ and $\sigma \longrightarrow$ zero. Another method of determining reflection coefficient by measuring transcellular osmosis is described below (p. 48).

3.10   Measurement of hydraulic conductivity

In the measurements of water potential and osmotic potential described above sufficient time must be allowed for the tissue to come to equilibrium with the external solution in order that the resistance of the plant tissue to water movement does not affect the measurement. However, like other materials, cell membranes do present a finite resistance to water movement even though it is low and it is of interest to know what this resistance, or hydraulic conductivity, L_p, may be. Usually it is only possible to measure hydraulic conductivity for the cell wall, plasmalemma, cytoplasm and tonoplast together in series. It is usually considered that the cell wall has a very high conductivity (low resistance) and that the measured L_p is of the cytoplasmic layer. However, there are cases, e.g. in suberized cells, where the resistance of the cell wall to water movement may be high so some care must be taken when interpreting results.

Methods of determining L_p are based on the equation $J_v = L_p \cdot \Delta\psi$, where J_v is the flux of water into the vacuole in cm^3 cm^{-2} s^{-1}; $\Delta\psi$ is the water potential difference in Pascals; L_p is in cm s^{-1} Pa^{-1}. Hydraulic conductivity is most easily determined in plasmolysed cells. A tissue is allowed to plasmolyse in a solution of given osmotic potential, ψ_{π_1}, and then transferred rapidly to another plasmolyticum with an osmotic potential of ψ_{π_2}. Water enters or leaves the plasmolysed vacuole depending on whether ψ_{π_2} is higher or lower than ψ_{π_1} and the plasmolysed protoplast swells or shrinks at a rate dependent on the magnitude of $(\psi_{\pi_1} - \psi_{\pi_2})$ and upon the value of L_p. Hydraulic conductivity can therefore be determined by observations of the rate of change in size of plasmolysed protoplasts when they are transferred from one solution to another.

Höfler used this method on a wide variety of cells and obtained values of L_p ranging from 0.5×10^{-9} to 2.0×10^{-8} cm s^{-1} kPa^{-1}.

It is likely that the hydraulic conductivity of the cytoplasmic layer in plasmolysed cells will be different from that in normal turgid cells and for this reason it is desirable to measure L_p in unplasmolysed cells to which the Höfler method is inapplicable. A method of determining L_p which can be used on the giant elongated cells of plants such as *Nitella* was devised by KAMIYA and TAZAWA (1956); this is the method of transcellular osmosis. The cell is placed in a double chamber with about one half on each side of a water-tight seal between the two compartments (Fig. 3–9). One chamber,

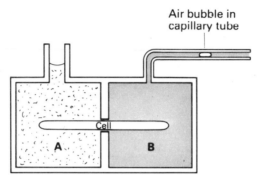

Fig. 3–9   Measurement of hydraulic conductivity by the method of transcellular osmosis. For explanation, see text.

A, is open and the other, B, is closed and has a capillary tube attached to it so that volume changes in that chamber can be measured accurately. At first the cell is allowed to equilibrate with tap water or dilute culture solution in both compartments at a constant temperature. The solution in A is then rapidly changed for a solution of mannitol or other slowly permeating solute at a non-plasmolysing concentration. The whole cell acts as a semi-permeable membrane and water begins to flow through it from the closed compartment into the open chamber at a rate which can be measured by observing the rate of movement of the air bubble. From the initial rate of flow J, L_p can be calculated from the equation

$$J = L_p \frac{A_1 A_2}{A_1 + A_2} \, \Delta\psi_\pi$$

where A_1 and A_2 are the areas of cell surface in each of the compartments and $\Delta\psi_\pi$ is the difference in osmotic potential between the two sides. This method has given values of 1–3×10^{-7} cm s^{-1} kPa^{-1} for cells from various members of the Characeae (DAINTY and GINZBERG, 1964). That is they are 10 to 100 times more permeable than the plasmolysed cells of parenchyma examined by Höfler.

Transcellular osmosis can also be used to measure the reflection coefficient. The rate of transport of water through the cell is measured first with a non-permeating solute and then with the solute whose reflection coefficient is to be measured. The ratio of the latter to the former gives the required value.

An ideal method of measuring hydraulic conductivity might appear to be by the use of water labelled with isotopes, deuterium (^{2}H) or tritium (^{3}H). If a tissue is equilibriated in heavy water and then transferred to ordinary water, the rate of exchange of water molecules can be estimated from the change in density. There are a number of problems with this technique.

(i) It has to be assumed that the rates of transport of heavy water molecules are the same as for ordinary water and that the labelled water does not interfere with the properties of the cell membranes.

(ii) The method depends on the cellular water and external medium being well mixed. This is not usually the case especially in plant cells and isotope exchange seems to be limited by the presence of unstirred layers of water, particularly in the cell wall. For these reasons, isotopes have not yet been satisfactorily applied to the measurement of hydraulic conductivity in plants.

3.11   Active water absorption

My mentor, the late Professor Bennet-Clark, F.R.S., and his students were among the first to observe that the mean osmotic potential of cell sap determined by the method of limiting plasmolysis is often significantly lower than that determined cryoscopically on sap extracted from the same tissue (Table 9). Dilution of vacuolar sap during extraction, penetration of plasmolyticum and neglect of matric potential are likely to be among the contributory factors. However, Bennet-Clark suggested that the discrepancy was an indication that water was being transported actively into plant cells by a mechanism that depends directly on metabolic energy (c.f. active transport of solutes). For some years this idea was taken quite seriously by plant physiologists until it was realized that because cytoplasm is very permeable to passive penetration of water an impossibly large amount of energy would be needed to pump water against existing diffusion gradients into the vacuoles of parenchyma cells. LEVITT (1947) calculated that the whole of the energy available from respiration in a red beetroot cell would be insufficient to maintain a gradient of water potential of more than about 100 kPa. It is now generally accepted that there is unlikely to be any significant active transport of water into the vacuoles of parenchyma cells. The possibility that water is actively transported in some specialized cells which may have low hydraulic conductivity is still not totally excluded (see below).

There is a considerable amount of evidence that water uptake by cells and tissues is somehow related to respiration and this has sometimes been taken to indicate that non-osmotic water absorption occurs. Aerobic conditions promote water uptake by roots and absorption is reduced at low temperature and by respiratory poisons. However, these treatments also affect the structure of cytoplasmic membranes and therefore may be expected to alter their hydraulic conductivity and this probably accounts for most of the effects observed. Moreover inhibition of respiration reduces the active transport of solutes into the vacuole which in turn may affect ψ_π, and hence indirectly the absorption of water.

Table 9   A comparison of the osmotic potentials, ψ_π, of vacuolar sap determined by cryoscopy, C, and by the method of limiting plasmolysis, LP. (Data from BENNET-CLARK, GREENWOOD and BARKER, 1936.)

			ψ_π (kPa)	
Tissue	Sample	C	LP	LP − C
Beta vulgaris	A	−1570	−2290	−720
(red beetroot) root	B	− 960	−1220	−260
	C	−1210	−1800	−590
Brassica hapobrassica	A	−1150	−1750	−600
(Swede) root	B	−1200	−1670	−470
Begonia sempervirens	A	− 540	− 780	−240
petiole	B	− 560	− 780	−220
Caladium bicolor	A	− 590	− 640	− 50
petiole	B	− 590	− 630	− 40

Some of the cases of apparent non-osmotic water movement can be explained by electro-osmosis (see p. 27). For example, when the trap of the insectivorous water plant, bladder-wort (*Utricularia* spp.), is being set (Fig. 3–10) water is removed from the bladder until the volume of the vesicle is reduced to as little as a half of its original size. This causes the wall of the bladder to cave in and a negative ψ_p is developed. When a small animal touches a hair on the door of the trap it springs open, releasing the tension and the victim is sucked into the bladder in a stream of water where it is later digested. There is an electrical potential difference between the internal and external solutions across the wall of the bladder (outside is negative by some 40–110 mv) and it is possible that water is transported out of the bladder by electro-osmosis (see p. 28).

Electro-osmosis has also been invoked to explain the observation that the coats of various seeds are more permeable to water in one direction than in the other. In support of this, BRAUNER (1930) observed that if the testa of horsechestnut (*Aesculus hippocastanum*) seeds is treated with potassium sulphate the electrical charge on the membrane and the polarity of water permeability are both reversed. However DAINTY (1963) thinks that

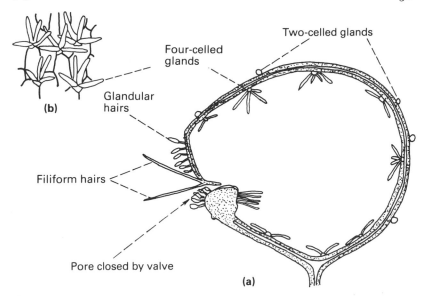

Fig. 3–10   (a) Longitudinal section through a bladder of *Utricularia* sp. (b) Surface of view of the inner wall of a bladder. (Redrawn from ARBER, 1925.)

differences in the rates of inward and outward flow of water through complex membranes might be caused simply by differences in hydration on the two sides.

Of great interest are the rather rapid changes in turgidity which occur in specialized 'motor' cells such as the 'hinge cells' in the upper surface of grass leaves which cause them to fold up under dry conditions, and the pulvinus cells of the sensitive plant, *Mimosa pudica*. Various workers have concluded that the rapid loss of turgidity which occurs in these cells is caused by active excretion of water. WEINTRAUB (1952) claimed that contractile vacuoles may be involved but although the importance of contractile vacuoles in regulating water content of some protozoa (e.g. *Amoeba*) and algae (e.g. *Chlamydomonas* spp.) is well known the existence of such organelles in higher plant cells has not yet been demonstrated convincingly. The rapid loss of turgor in motor cells of *Mimosa pudica* is accompanied by a massive efflux of potassium (cf. loss of potassium from guard cells during stomatal closure, see Chapter 4) and the loss of water is almost certainly caused by a sudden increase in the permeability of cell membranes to ions.

The excretion of water by hydathodes and other glands is thought to be a passive process resulting either from the development of hydrostatic pressure in the cells (see Chapter 6) or by active excretion of solutes.

3.12   Water relations of growing cells

This chapter has been concerned so far with reversible changes that occur in the water content of mature cells when they are transferred from one environment to another. Only in cases where stretching of the cell walls leads to plastic deformation and hence a change in the elasticity coefficient is a permanent change in water content induced. The situation is quite different in growing cells where an equilibrium is only established after a prolonged period of time when growth eventually stops.

Some people have the mistaken impression that the force which causes a cell to enlarge is turgor pressure and that the cell is blown up rather like a balloon or a pneumatic tyre. This idea was fostered in the 1950s by the suggestions of eminent plant physiologists, such as K. V. Thimann and J. Bonner, that the auxin, indol-3-ylacetic acid (IAA) which stimulates cell expansion, acts by promoting the active pumping of water into them. Although this idea was soon dropped, when the concept of active transport of water was found to be untenable, many current textbooks of plant physiology still give the erroneous impression that turgor pressure is responsible for cell enlargement as BURSTRÖM (1971a) has recently pointed out. It is true that a cell can not grow unless it is turgid, but there is no quantitative correlation between rates of growth and turgor pressure. In general, turgor pressure tends to be lower in cells which are growing rapidly than in those growing more slowly and this is the opposite of what would be expected if turgor pressure was the force responsible for growth.

Water enters a growing cell for the same reason that it goes into a flaccid non-growing cell, namely because there is a water potential gradient between the vacuolar sap and external solution. This gradient is maintained while a cell is growing, because growth of the wall prevents ψ_p from rising as quickly as it would do otherwise. It is now generally accepted that the role of IAA in regulating cell enlargement is in controlling wall growth. There is also the possibility that ψ_π may be lowered in a growing cell by accumulation of solutes, but this is of secondary importance. Experimental evidence indicates that in a rapidly growing cell, e.g. in the extending zone of a root, ψ_π actually rises during the most rapid period of growth, because water is being taken up more quickly than solutes, and that ψ_p is a more important factor regulating ψ_v than is ψ_π at this stage. As growth of the cell wall in surface area begins to decline, and it becomes thicker, ψ_p begins to increase more rapidly until equilibrium is established in the mature cell.

4 Stomatal Movement

4.1 Structure of stomata

The epidermis of the aerial parts of vascular plants is perforated by small pores, the stomata (singular stoma) through which gaseous exchange occurs (Fig. 4–1). They occur most abundantly on leaves but are also found on stems, flowers, and on some fruits. In angiosperms they are located mainly on the lower surface of leaves and in most trees and shrubs they are absent from the upper surfaces altogether, a condition which is referred to as hypostomy. Water plants with floating leaves, such as water-lilies, have stomata on the upper surface only of these leaves (epistomy) and they are either absent or rudimentary on submerged leaves. Most herbaceous plants have stomata on both surfaces (that is, they are amphistomous) and in many, especially in grasses, the numbers on the two surfaces are approximately the same (Table 10).

Stomata are formed before a leaf has completed most of its enlargement and since the number of stomata per leaf does not change much during leaf expansion they are much closer together in a young leaf than in an older one. The figures quoted in Table 10 are for fully expanded leaves.

Table 10 Approximate size and distribution of stomata on mature leaves of various plants.

Species	Mean stomatal no. mm^{-2}		Mean size when fully open (length and breadth, μm)	Mean distance apart on lower epidermis (μm)
	Upper epidermis	Lower epidermis		
Bean (*Phaseolus vulgaris*)	40	281	7×3	68
Sunflower (*Helianthus annuus*)	85	156	38×7	91
Ivy (*Hedera helix*)	0	158	11×4	90
Tomato (*Lycopersicon esculentum*)	12	130	13×6	99
Geranium (*Pelargonium* sp.)	19	59	24×9	146
Maize (*Zea mays*)	52	68	19×5	137
Oat (*Avena sativa*)	25	23	38×8	236
Wheat (*Triticum* sp.)	33	14	18×7	302
Wandering Jew (*Zebrina pendula*)	0	14	31×12	302

54

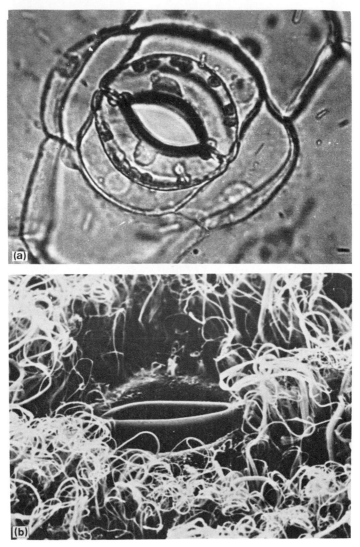

Fig. 4-1 (a) An open stoma of *Commelina communis*. Note the position of chloroplasts in the guard cells, adjacent to the cell wall near the subsidiary cells. The stoma is about half open. (From MANSFIELD, 1976.) (b) Partly-open stoma on the under-surface of a banana leaf. Note the curled threads of wax protruding from the cuticle except over the guard cells. (The photograph was taken by Dr P. J. Holloway and Mr E. A. Baker of Long Ashton Research Station, Bristol, and is reproduced from GUNNING and STEER (1975). *Plant Cell Biology: An Ultra-structural Approach*, Edward Arnold, London, by kind permission of the authors and publisher.)

Although the numbers of stomata per mm² of leaf surface may look small the total number on a plant is usually enormous and commonly runs into many millions. In general, the number of stomata per unit of leaf surface area is higher in dry conditions than when plants are grown at high humidity. This is attributed mainly to a reduction in leaf expansion in water-stressed plants, but the number of stomata expressed as a percentage of the number of epidermal cells (the 'stomatal index') also tends to be lower when plants are well supplied with water, and in the extreme case of submerged leaves there may be no stomata at all. On the other hand, individual stomata tend to be larger in plants of moist habitats. Abnormally, large stomata occur together with normal sized ones in many plants, and it is through these water pores, which are often permanently open, that guttation commonly occurs (see p. 102).

A stoma arises as a split in the middle lamella between two adjoining 'guard' cells, each of which is formed by unequal division of an epidermal cell. The larger portion usually becomes a 'subsidiary' cell, which sometimes divides again to produce a complex of three or more subsidiary cells around the stomata (Fig. 4–2b).

The guard-cells in most dicotyledons, and in some monocotyledons, e.g. *Allium cepa*, are typically sausage-shaped and joined together at the ends with an elliptical pore between them (Fig. 4–1a and Fig. 4–2d). The cell walls are unevenly thickened and often the dorsal wall (the one away from the pore) is thinner and more easily stretched than the central wall. Thus when the guard cells become more turgid their shape changes; the dorsal walls become more convex, causing the central walls to become concave and opening the pore (Fig. 4–2d, B). Conversely, when the guard cells become less turgid the pore closes (Fig. 4–2d, A). Guard-cells are unusual in the extent to which their volume increases when they become turgid. In contrast to ordinary parenchyma cells and epidermal cells which commonly increase in volume by about 5–15% between incipient plasmolysis and full turgidity (see Fig. 3–2) guard cells may enlarge by 50% or more. This is attributable to the very high elastic coefficient of guard cell walls (see p. 46). Changes in the turgidity of subsidiary cells sometimes contribute to the control of stomatal aperture. In contrast to the situation in guard cells, high turgidity in subsidiary cells tends to induce stomatal closure rather than opening.

The guard cells of many monocotyledons, including grasses and sedges are dumb-bell shaped, with a narrow cylindrical region in which the cell wall is thickened, and dilated ends with thin cell walls. In these plants the subsidiary cells are often much more prominent than the guard cells, and in contrast with the rather random arrangements found in dicotyledons, the stomata tend to be arranged in parallel rows mainly over the veins (Fig. 4–2c). The size of the pore is again regulated by the turgidity of the guard cells. When the cells take up water the ends of each cell swell and the thickened regions are drawn apart. In some cases (e.g. wheat) when a

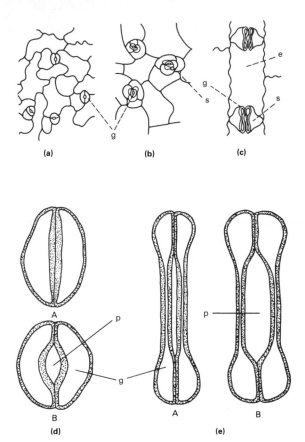

Fig. 4–2 Morphology of stomata. (a) *Tropaeolum* (no subsidiary cells); (b) *Sedum* (three subsidiary cells of unequal size surrounding each stoma); (c) *Zea* (dumb-bell shaped guard cells and paired subsidiary cells typical of grasses); (d) *Allium* stoma in the closed (A) and open (B) position; (e) 'Grasstype' stoma in the closed (A) and open (B) position.
g = guard cell; s = subsidiary cell; e = epidermal cell; p = pore.

stoma is fully open the narrow region is bent into a semi-circle and the pore becomes almost round.

4.2 Measurement of stomatal size

To study the operation of guard cells it is often necessary to measure the size of the pore under various environmental conditions. This is not very easy to do accurately because of the small size of stomata and their sensitivity to handling. Lightly touching, or even breathing on a leaf with open stomata is liable to make them close almost at once. Nevertheless, the following methods have been found to give satisfactory results in the hands of experienced investigators.

4.2.1   Direct microscopic observation

The material is placed under a microscope and the dimensions of the pores measured using an eye-piece micrometer. It is rarely possible to study the surface of an intact leaf attached to a plant in this way and more often the leaf is detached and cut up into pieces before examination. Strips of epidermis in which the guard cells may still be functional are often used in research on stomatal physiology and pore sizes can sometimes be measured by direct microscopic observation of such strips placed on a microscope slide. Microscopic observation of stomata on either leaves or epidermal strips is impossible, however, if the leaf surface is covered by hairs or scales or if the stomata are sunk in pits.

Another problem with direct microscopic observation is that because of variation in pore aperture between individual stomata, a large number has to be measured to get a reliable average value and this takes such a long time that pore size may have changed before the measurements are completed. This difficulty can be overcome by photographing the leaf surface under the microscope and making the measurements at leisure on suitably enlarged prints. An alternative approach is to coat the leaf with a substance such as collodion, cellulose acetate, or a dental plastic, which solidifies to form an impression of the leaf surface. Measurements can then be made microscopically on a photograph either of the mould itself or of a positive replica.

Various methods have been used to 'fix' stomata for subsequent microscopic examination. For example, strips of leaf epidermis may be removed and plunged quickly into absolute ethanol (LLOYD, 1908). Such methods give reliable results only for leaves which have an easily detachable epidermis and can be misleading especially with widely-open stomata which may begin to close very quickly.

4.2.2   Infiltration methods

If a drop of liquid of sufficiently low surface tension is applied to the surface of a leaf with open stomata it penetrates into the intercellular spaces and the infiltrated area appears translucent. Thus by examining the degree of penetration of a series of liquids with a range of surface tensions it is possible to estimate the size of the stomata. A useful series is medicinal paraffin, absolute ethanol, benzol, and xylol. The first only penetrates large, wide-open stomata, and the last all except those that are almost closed. Graded mixtures of two liquids such as medicinal paraffin and xylol in the proportions, 10 : 0, 9 : 1 . . . 0 : 10, have also been used successfully.

As an alternative procedure a single liquid can be applied and the leaf area injected in a given time measured. When the stomata are fully open penetration occurs more rapidly than when they are nearly closed. If a dye such as gentian violet is added to the penetrating liquid the area injected can be estimated more easily. WILLIAMS (1949) found that this method worked well for *Pelargonium* leaves and the area of injected regions can be measured some time later even on dried pressed leaves.

An advantage of the infiltration method over direct microscopic examination is that it gives a value for the mean size of thousands of stomata from a single observation. However, to obtain absolute values for pore size the method must be calibrated for a given species against actual pore sizes measured by one of the methods described in section 4.2.1. If only relative sizes are needed this will not be necessary.

4.2.3   *Porometers*

The size of stomata can also be measured by their resistance to either bulk flow or diffusion of gas, e.g. air, through them. A simple air flow porometer, that is often used in schools is shown in Fig. 4–3. A small chamber is attached by an air-tight joint to the leaf surface and air is drawn from it by a pressure difference caused by a water column in a graduated tube. The water meniscus is set to a given height by applying suction through the open end of the T tube and the tube is then sealed with a spring clip. The rate at which the water meniscus falls depends on the pressure gradient and on the resistance offered by the stomata through which air passes into the cup. If the leaf is amphistomous it is best to attach the cup to the surface on which there are fewer stomata. Most of the air then passes vertically through the leaf and resistance to lateral flow of air is minimal. If the stomata occur only on one surface the porometer must of course be fixed on that side and air will have to travel laterally through the leaf from stomata outside the cup thus increasing the resistance measured, since it will include a longer pathway through the leaf mesophyll.

Various modifications have been devised to improve the accuracy and convenience of air-flow porometers. These include a constant pressure porometer (KNIGHT, 1915) which employs suction to maintain a pressure gradient and thus overcomes the disadvantage of having a decreasing pressure difference as the water column falls. MEIDNER (1965) and SHIMSHI (1977) have designed simple porometers for use in the field; the original articles should be consulted for details of their construction.

Physiologists are generally interested not so much in the resistance (or conductance) of stomata to mass flow of air, since this does not occur normally in a leaf, but in the resistance to diffusion. Although diffusive resistance can be calculated from measurements of resistance to mass flow this is not always easy and attempts have been made to devise porometers which estimate diffusive resistance directly. In general, these involve measurements of the rate at which a gas, e.g. hydrogen, diffuses from one side of a leaf to the other (see, e.g. SPANNER, 1953, and STILES, 1970; various

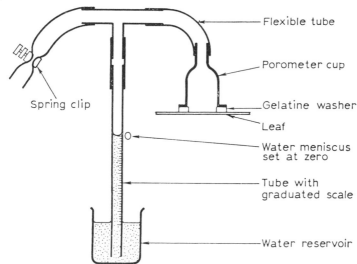

Fig. 4–3   A simple porometer based on a design by DARWIN and PERTZ (1911). For explanation, see text.

designs of diffusive porometers for use both in the laboratory and in the field are now available commercially).

Porometer measurements like the infiltration method, have the advantage of integrating the resistance of many stomata. If it is required to relate resistance, whether to diffusion or mass flow, to stomatal size, it is again necessary to calibrate the instrument for a particular leaf by direct microscopic observation of stomatal size.

A problem with porometers is that the presence of the porometer cup on the leaf surface may alter the size of the stomata beneath it by reducing light intensity or by altering the temperature or the CO_2 concentration within the cup (see section 4.3). In order to minimize this difficulty the cup must be removed in the intervals between porometer readings when experiments are prolonged.

4.2.4   Transpiration measurement

Under conditions in which the rate of transpiration is controlled by stomatal resistance, measurement of transpiration by methods such as those described in Chapter 5 can be used to estimate the size of stomata. Such methods can be looked upon as diffusive porometry, in which the diffusing gas is water vapour leaving the leaf. The well-known cobalt chloride paper method (p. 70) has sometimes been used to measure stomatal apertures as well as transpiration. The danger in using this method for the measurement of stomatal resistance is that the shading effect of the paper on the leaf surface may alter the size of the stomata beneath it, so that they are no longer representative of the condition of stomata in the leaf as a whole.

4.3   Factors affecting stomatal size

Guard cells are peculiar among plant cells in their extreme sensitivity to environmental stimuli and in the speed at which turgidity changes occur. Closed stomata begin to open in a few minutes after exposure to light and they may start to close again when returned to the dark in a matter of seconds. Apart from light, the most important factors influencing the turgidity of guard cells, and hence the size of stomata, are CO_2 concentration, temperature and water supply (Fig. 4–4). As a result of various interactions between these influences several diurnal patterns of stomatal behaviour occur. In most thin-leaved mesophytes, when adequately supplied with water, the stomata open quickly soon after sunrise and remain so for the greater part of the day. Sometimes they close temporarily about midday and open again for a period in the afternoon; in other species, e.g. many cereals, the stomata are open only for a few hours in the morning and do not open again until next day. In most plants the stomata are partially closed well before sunset. They

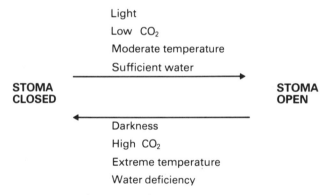

Fig. 4–4   Usual response of stomata to environmental factors.

usually remain closed until dawn but sometimes there is a brief opening period during the night especially in those plants in which closure occurs early in the day.

In some xerophytes belonging to the family Crassulaceae the stomata often open only at night. These plants also have a different form of metabolism (Crassulacean Acid Metabolism) by which CO_2 is assimilated in the dark and used in the synthesis of organic acids such as malic acid. These acids are subsequently converted to sugars in the light, releasing CO_2 in the leaf cells which can then be used in photosynthesis while the stomata are closed. As a result water is conserved during the day when the temperature is high and evaporation rapid.

4.3.1   *Response to CO$_2$*

When plants are put in CO_2-free air, stomata tend to open even in the dark. Conversely, an increase in CO_2 concentration above that normally present in air ($\simeq 0.03\%$) causes stomata to close in the light. There are indications that the CO_2 concentration in the intercellular spaces of the leaf in the vicinity of a stoma is of greater significance than that elsewhere in the leaf or in the air outside. When the stomata of a plant have been closed by exposure to high CO_2, they do not re-open readily if transferred to CO_2-free air in the dark, presumably because the CO_2 level in the intercellular spaces remains high. Evidently the outer walls of the guard cells are not very permeable to CO_2, possibly because they are covered by cuticle. If the plant is illuminated, re-opening occurs when the level of CO_2 within the leaf has been reduced sufficiently by photosynthesis.

It has been observed that the opening stimulus can be transmitted from an illuminated to a darkened part of a leaf. This probably occurs because of the establishment of a gradient of CO_2 concentration between photosynthesizing and non-photosynthesizing tissues which results in a gradual reduction in the CO_2 levels in the intercellular spaces of the darkened part. Stomata in the non-chlorophyllous regions of variegated leaves respond on exposure to light or darkness in the same way as those in green parts, but do so more slowly. This is attributed to a delay in the alteration of CO_2 level in the intercellular spaces of the non-photosynthetic tissues.

4.3.2   *Response to temperature*

Within the range of about 5–25°C the effect of temperature is mainly on the rate of the opening and closing reactions rather than on aperture size. At low temperatures stomata behave sluggishly and with increasing temperature movement occurs more quickly. Temperatures above about 25°C cause closure in a number of plants and this is thought to be the reason for the mid-day closure observed in certain tropical species, e.g. coffee (*Coffea arabica*). HEATH and ORCHARD (1957) attributed mid-day closure to accumulation of CO_2 in the intercellular spaces of the leaf as a result of stimulated respiration and reduced photosynthesis at high temperature. MEIDNER and HEATH (1959) found that high temperature (35°C) closure in onion (*Allium cepa*) could be prevented if the hollow cavity of the leaf was swept with CO_2-free air. Under these conditions, opening of closed stomata on exposure to light actually occurred more quickly at 35°C than at 26°C.

4.3.3   Response to water stress

If a plant is losing more water through transpiration than it is absorbing by the roots a water deficit develops and this usually causes stomatal closure irrespective of light, temperature or carbon dioxide concentration (Fig. 4–4). When a leaf wilts rapidly there may be an opening response before the stomata close. This could be due to a more rapid initial loss of water by the subsidiary and surrounding epidermal cells than by the guard cells causing the guard cells to swell temporarily due to a decrease in ψ_p (see p. 37). A greater loss of turgidity in the adjacent cells than in the guard cells is thought to be responsible also for the permanent opening of stomata which sometimes occurs when wilting is extreme.

It has been reported that sometimes the stomata in wilted plants remain closed, or do not open fully, for several days after the leaves have recovered their turgor. As opening cannot be stimulated during this period by flushing the leaves with CO_2-free air it is unlikely that CO_2 is involved in this effect. WRIGHT and HIRON (1969) found that wilted wheat leaves have a higher content of abscisic acid (ABA) than normal and that upon recovery the ABA disappears quite slowly over a period of days. It has been shown that ABA supplied to the leaves of various plants causes stomata to close and it seems likely that naturally-produced ABA is involved in short-term stomatal responses to water stress (see below).

4.3.4   Autonomous rhythms of stomatal movement

Stomatal regulation is one of many activities of plants that show endogenous circadian rhythms, i.e. rhythms that occur at least for a time even under constant environment conditions with a periodicity of about a day. An example of such autonomous behaviour of stomata is shown in Fig. 4–5. This rhythm is presumably imposed on the plant by regular alternation of light and darkness and it gradually disappears if plants are kept in continuous light or dark. The phase appears to be set by the time of change from darkness to light and can be reset after plants have been kept for a time in the dark by a brief exposure to light.

FRANCIS DARWIN (1898) observed that stomata tend to close more rapidly when darkened during the afternoon than in the morning and conversely open more rapidly in the morning after a period of darkness than if the onset of illumination is delayed until the afternoon. These differences in the rates of response may be correlated with the endogenous rhythms of opening and closing observed under constant conditions. It should be pointed out that respiration of leaves in the dark also shows circadian periodicity and it is possible that the rhythm of stomatal movement may be brought about by rhythmic changes in CO_2 concentration within the leaf.

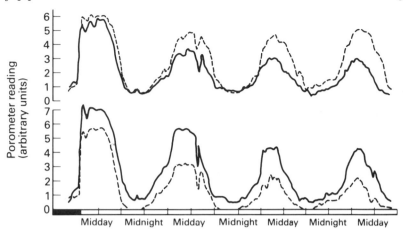

Fig. 4–5 Changes in stomatal aperture on two plants of *Tradescantia virginiana* in continuous light (1500 lux). The continuous and broken lines are recordings of stomatal aperture on two separate leaves of the same plant. (Redrawn from MARTIN and MEIDNER, 1971.)

4.4   The mechanism of stomatal movement

4.4.1   *Control of* ψ_{cell}

Water enters guard cells, causing stomata to open, when their water potential is lower (more negative) than that of the surroundings, and when the potential gradient is reversed, the stomata close. Water potential may be changed by alterations in ψ_m, ψ_p or ψ_π (see Chapter 3). ψ_m has never been measured in guard cells and so its value is unknown but this has not prevented some people from suggesting that increased hydration of cytoplasmic colloids might be a factor in the uptake of water by guard cells in the light. Direct measurements of ψ_p have been made by EDWARDS and MEIDNER (1975), and HALL and KAUFMANN (1975) have postulated that mid-day closure may be due in part to a direct effect of a decrease in atmospheric humidity on the elasticity of guard cell walls. If ϵ is reduced, ψ_p will increase and ψ_{cell} rise causing closure; conversely an increase in ϵ will lead to reduction of ψ_p, increase uptake of water, and opening. In view of the unusual properties of guard cell walls and their known role in controlling cell shape it is quite plausible that reversible changes in cell wall structure causing alterations in ϵ and hence ψ_p may play a part in the control of water potential in guard cells and hence stomatal size.

4.4.2   Control of ψ_π

Most attention has been given to the possibility that water potential is controlled by changes in ψ_π and there is no doubt that this is an important factor in stomatal movement. Guard cells differ from other epidermal cells in that they contain chloroplasts (Fig. 4–1a) and an early hypothesis of stomatal opening put forward by H. von Mohl was that photosynthesis causes an increase in turgor in the guard cells by accumulation of sugars in the vacuoles. It was not until nearly 100 years later that it was confirmed by the use of radioactive ^{14}C-labelled CO_2 that guard cells are capable of photosynthesis, but that it occurs much too slowly to account for the osmotic potential changes necessary to cause opening at the rates observed (SHAW and MACLACHLAN, 1954).

4.4.3   The starch-sugar hypothesis

Long before this, others had suspected that accumulation of the products of photosynthesis in guard cells is insufficient to account for stomatal movement, and LLOYD (1908) put forward the idea that the turgidity of guard cells is controlled mainly by the interconversion of starch and sugar. He observed, and others, e.g. SAYRE (1926) and SCARTH (1932), confirmed that starch grains tend to disappear when stomata open and re-appear when they close. The accumulation of starch in guard cells in the dark and its disappearance in the light is the opposite of what happens in mesophyll cells and in ordinary epidermal cells.

Scarth showed that guard cell sap had a pH value of 6–7 when stomata were open compared with 4–5 when they were closed. From these observations he concluded that stomatal opening in the light is caused by an increase in pH which favours the hydrolysis of starch to sugar in the guard cells and thus lowers the osmotic potential. He suggested that light might instigate these changes by removing carbonic acid from the guard cells through photosynthesis.

Following the demonstration by HANES (1940) that the enzyme, starch phosphorylase, catalysing the reaction:

$$\text{Starch} + n \text{ (inorganic phosphate)} \to n \text{ (glucose-1-phosphate)}$$

occurs in plant tissues, it was concluded that this enzyme is involved in the starch-sugar interconversion in guard cells and that whereas a slightly acid pH (6–7) favours production of sugar phosphate, the reverse reaction is favoured at pH 4–5. YIN and TUNG (1948) showed that the enzyme actually occurs in guard cells. It should be noted that the phosphorylase reaction alone does not cause the required change in osmotic potential because for each molecule of glucose-1-phosphate (G-1-P) produced an ion of inorganic phosphate disappears, and as n is a large number the total number of particles in the solution hardly changes at all. However, if by further reactions the G-1-P is hydrolysed to glucose, and inorganic phosphate released, a large decrease in osmotic potential will occur.

Although there is much evidence which supports the starch-sugar hypothesis, it must be emphasized that starch content and degree of stomatal opening are not always very closely correlated, and sometimes, e.g. during mid-day closure, no change in starch content seems to occur. There are some guard cells, e.g. those of the onion, that do not store starch, but in such cases other polysaccharides, e.g. fructosans, may fulfil a similar function. The greatest weakness of the starch-sugar hypothesis is that the concomitant increase in sugar content associated with starch hydrolysis, which is believed to be the cause of the lowering of ψ_π, has never been demonstrated.

Another criticism is that the changes in CO_2 concentrations observed (say from about 0.03% to 0.01%) are insufficient to cause the observed change in acidity which may be as much as two pH units. It has been suggested that CO_2 may be converted in the guard cells into carboxylic acids ($R.COOH$) which affect the acidity of the cell much more than does CO_2 itself. In fact, the level of such acids (mainly malic acid) is higher in guard cells when the stomata are open than when they are closed (ALLAWAY, 1973). The acids are probably formed from starch or other stored carbohydrates rather than by CO_2 fixation (see below).

4.4.4   The ion accumulation hypothesis

The accumulation of K^+ ions in guard cells of open stomata was demonstrated by MACALLUM (1905) using a histochemical method, but this observation aroused little interest until a Japanese worker, FUJINO (1967), suggested that a light-activated K^+ accumulation in guard cells could play a major role in the mechanism of stomatal opening. FISCHER and HSIAO (1968) showed that there was indeed a quantitative relationship between the amount of $^{86}Rb^+$ (used as a tracer for K^+) taken up by guard cells of *Vicia faba* epidermal strips, and the degree of opening of the stomata. It was calculated that accumulation of K^+ with an associated anion could account for the observed decrease in ψ_π of the guard cells during stomatal opening. Other cations (e.g. Na^+, Ca^{++}) were accumulated to a much smaller extent than K^+ and produced a smaller opening response. The nature of the associated anion in the external solution appeared to be relatively unimportant.

Measurement of the amounts of potassium, chlorine and phosphorus present in guard cells of *Vicia faba* leaves using the method of electron-probe micro-analysis indicates that Cl^- and phosphate accumulate to a lesser extent than K^+ in the guard cells of open stomata (HUMBLE and RASCHKE, 1971), the excess K^+ being mainly associated with malate. This seems to be the case in some other species, but not in all. In *Zea mays*, for example, Cl^- balances about 40% of the K^+ in the guard cells of open stomata (RASCHKE and FELLOWS, 1971).

In the guard cells of some plants, e.g. tobacco, Na^+ seems to be accumulated in preference to K^+ and this is also the case in some succulents, e.g. *Kalanchoe marmorata*, in which the stomata open at night, and possibly in halophytes. It has been proposed that in those species in which stomata open during the day, K^+ (or Na^+) is accumulated by a light-activated cation carrier mechanism energized by ATP. When the cation is accumulated as malate, the malic acid is derived from starch and cation uptake involves exchange with H^+. On the other hand, if cations are taken up in association with anions such as Cl^- from the surroundings, malate does not accumulate and any starch that disappears is presumably converted mainly to sugar. In darkness, the cation pump stops, and the accumulated ions either leak out of the cells, or are actively excreted across the plasma membrane. Any malate present is reconverted to starch and the lost cations must be replaced by H^+. In succulents where stomata open in the dark the light-activated cation pump apparently transports ions out of the cells while an inwardly-directed carrier operates in the dark. In this case the energy required for ion accumulation must come from respiration, but light-activated pumps may be energized partly by photosynthesis in the guard cell chloroplasts. ABA appears to cause stomata to close by inhibiting the cation influx pumps and possibly stimulating efflux, whereas certain phytotoxins, e.g. fusicoccin, have the opposite effects. These substances, which are produced by pathogenic fungi, cause wilting by inducing the stomata to open more widely than normal under conditions of water stress (see Chapter 5).

The inorganic ions that are accumulated in guard cells during opening are believed to come from the subsidiary cells either through plasmodesmata or via the cell walls, and presumably they return there along the same pathways when the stomata close. It is evident therefore that subsidiary cells behave in the opposite way to guard cells, releasing ions when the latter are accumulating them and vice versa. The reason for this difference in response which may be related to the different effects of light on the starch-sugar balance in the two types of cell is unknown. BOWLING (1976) has suggested that the malate accumulating in guard cells may be transported from subsidiary cells rather than synthesized *in situ*, but TRAVIS and MANSFIELD (1977) showed that malate accumulates in guard cells in epidermal strips in which the other epidermal cells have been killed, so that transport from subsidiary cells cannot be an essential part of the stomatal mechanism at least in the species studied (*Commelina communis*).

A summary of the changes that may occur in guard cells of *Vicia faba* during stomatal opening in the light and closure in the dark is shown in Fig. 4–6. There are a number of points about the mechanism which still remain to be clarified, for example, we do not know yet exactly how light acts in promoting ion accumulation and how this is related to the disappearance of starch, and the changes in CO_2 concentration and pH

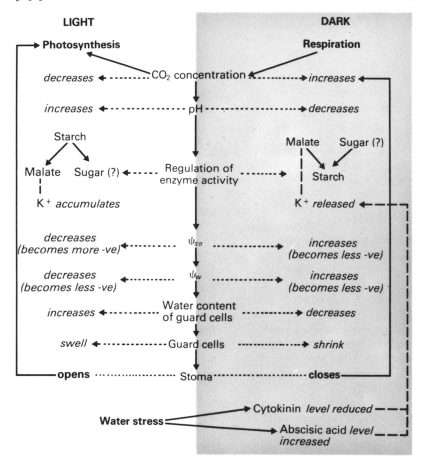

Fig. 4–6   Changes associated with stomatal movement in *Vicia faba*.

that occur. The way in which the changes in the levels of growth substances, such as cytokinins and abscisic acid, influence the system is also hypothetical. It is evident that guard cells are quite remarkable structures with many jealously-guarded secrets that remain to be revealed.

5 Transpiration

5.1 Measurements of transpiration rate

That a plant gives off water vapour can be demonstrated quite simply by watering it well and putting its leaves in an enclosed space, e.g. under a bell-jar, when water will condense on the sides of the vessel. Stephen HALES, some time vicar of Teddington, near London, who was one of the first men to study the physiology of plants quantitatively, described such an experiment in his book *Vegetable Staticks* (1727) which makes entertaining reading and has been republished as a new edition recently (1961). Hales devised a variety of methods of measuring the amount of water lost by a plant in a given time and these same basic methods are still in use today. Although the techniques employed have been refined in the intervening years an underlying difficulty still remains, namely that placing a plant under conditions necessary for measurement affects the transpiration rate to a greater or lesser extent because it is so sensitive to environmental conditions, such as light intensity, air movement and humidity. The various methods available are as follows:

5.1.1 Loss in weight of a potted plant

As Hales showed, the transpiration rate of a potted plant can be estimated by measuring the loss in weight of the plant and its container over a period of time. It is necessary to prevent evaporation from the soil by covering it with waterproof material, and if a clay pot is used, this must also be enclosed. It is necessary to employ a fairly large quantity of soil to prevent it drying out too much during prolonged experiments, and to supply additional water at intervals. It is not unusual for a plant under favourable conditions to lose the equivalent of its own weight of water in a single day. With suitable weighing equipment it is possible to measure the transpiration of young trees growing in vessels containing 500 kg or more of soil, but the method is obviously more suitable for small plants. It can be adapted for use with plants growing in solution culture as well as in soil, but there are problems if the solution needs to be aerated.

An inherent error in this method is that the loss of water through transpiration is partly offset by an increase in weight of the plant as a result of growth and so the estimates of water loss are inevitably too low. However, this error is usually less than those associated with weighing and, except when plants are transpiring very slowly and growing fast, can safely be neglected.

5.1.2 *Loss in weight of excised shoots or leaves*

A leaf or leafy branch is cut off and weighed on a sensitive balance at intervals of one or two minutes. The results are plotted graphically and the line joining the points is extrapolated to zero time. The initial slope of the line is taken to represent the transpiration rate immediately before excision (Fig. 5–1). The method gives a satisfactory estimate of water loss

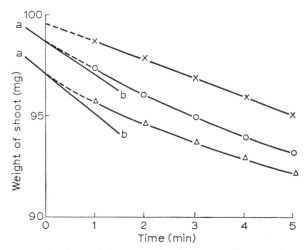

Fig. 5–1 Determination of the transpiration rate of a cut shoot by rapid weighing at short intervals. X——X, O——O, △——△, are measurements made on different shoots. When the graph is curved the initial slope is calculated by drawing a tangent (a-b) to the curve at zero time.

from the material *in situ* if environmental conditions remain the same during weighing and as long as the plant is not suffering from water stress. If an appreciable water deficit exists within the plant there is an immediate increase in transpiration rate upon excision due to release of tensions in the xylem vessels (see below) and this can cause serious errors. Nevertheless, the method has been used widely, particularly in ecological work and has provided reliable comparative data (Table 11). IDLE (1976) has devised an electrical weight transducer which is less expensive than a balance of comparable sensitivity and easier to use.

5.1.3 *Freeman's method* (FREEMAN, 1908)

The aerial portion of a plant, or a part of it is enclosed in a glass vessel through which a stream of dry air is allowed to flow. The water vapour is collected in tared tubes containing phosphorus pentoxide or calcium chloride and weighed. In a control experiment the same volume of air is drawn through a similar apparatus without the plant, and from the

Table 11   Relative rates (Spruce = 100) of transpiration of various trees estimated by different investigators using two methods. (From HUBER, 1953.)

Species	Weighing of potted seedlings (Eidmann)	Rapid weighing of detached twigs	
		(Pisek and Cantelliere)	(Polster)
Spruce (Picea abies)	100	100	100
Scots pine (Pinus sylvestris)	181	133	139
Larch (Larix europaea)	310	212	212
Beech (Fagus sylvatica)	268	377	372
Oak (Quercus robur)	286	512	460
Birch (Betula verrucosa)	618	541	740

changes in weight of the two sets of collecting tubes the amount of water transpired by the plant in a given time is determined.

More recently, various kinds of hygrometers have been used to monitor the water content of the air after it has passed over the plant. These include the use of wet and dry bulb thermometers and thermocouples, measurement of infra-red absorption (SCARTH, LOEWY and SHAW, 1948) and the corona hygrometer (ANDERSSON, HERTZ and RUFELT, 1954). FALK (1966) has described a sensitive hygrometer which makes use of microwaves to determine changes in the dielectric properties of the air associated with changes of humidity.

The basic method has several serious disadvantages. In particular the experimental material is placed in a closed container under abnormal conditions of light intensity, temperature and humidity. Transpiration is also affected by the rate of air-flow; when the flow of air is rapid, humidity remains low and transpiration is maximal, while with a slow airstream humidity rises and transpiration is reduced. Therefore the results are only valid for the conditions to which the transpiring material is exposed during the measurments but the method has been very useful for studying the quantitative effect of such factors as wind-speed, temperature, CO_2 concentration and the CO_2 humidity of the air on transpiration rates.

5.1.4   Use of colour indicator papers

Pieces of filter paper soaked in a concentrated (3–5%) solution of cobalt chloride or cobalt thiocyanate are dried in an oven until they appear blue. When such paper absorbs moisture the blue colour fades and gradually changes to pink. To measure transpiration a dry piece of paper is placed on the leaf surface and held in place by two thin pieces of glass (microscope cover slips are very suitable) clipped above and below the leaf. Moisture from the outside air should be excluded by sealing round the glass above the paper with petroleum jelly or silicone grease. The time taken for the colour of the paper to change from one standard shade of blue to another is a measure of the amount of water lost by the part of the leaf covered by the paper. The method is basically the same as that used to measure dampness in the walls of buildings, and humidity kits sold for this purpose can be adapted for determination of the transpiration rate of leaves.

The colour indicator method is useful for comparative purposes, e.g. for comparing transpiration rates between two sides of the same leaf or two leaves of the same plant, but often gives a poor estimation of the transpiration rate of the whole plant. This is because the technique measures transpiration rate from a leaf surface placed under very artificial conditions. Light intensity is reduced because of the paper, while the air is still, and almost dry. The method can be used to estimate stomatal resistance but there is a danger that when the paper is applied the stomata covered will close very quickly (see p. 59).

5.1.5   Infra-red absorption

A sophisticated method of estimating transpiration is to pass an infra-red beam through a leaf and measure its intensity on the other side by means of a small infra-red sensitive photocell. An increase in the density or thickness of the boundary layer containing water vapour, which absorbs infra-red radiation, decreases the amount of radiation received by the detector and vice versa. The technique cannot easily be calibrated to measure absolute transpiration rates but it is useful for detecting changes in rate as a result of changes in the environment, e.g. the effect of wind-speed.

5.1.6   Potometers

With a potometer (literally: 'drink measurer'; not to be confused with porometer, Fig. 4–3) the rate of water loss from a plant or cut shoot is determined indirectly by measuring the rate of absorption, making the assumption that absorption balances the water lost in transpiration. One form of the apparatus consists essentially of a water reservoir into which the plant or its part is sealed and to which a glass capillary tube of known bore is attached (Fig. 5–2). A bubble of air is introduced into the tube and its rate of movement across a scale is used as an indication of the rate of transpiration. If the bore of the tube is known the amount of water absorbed in a given time can be calculated.

A number of different designs of potometers have been used with varying success with both cut shoots and whole plants. Except when experiments are performed at a constant temperature it is desirable to have a control potometer set up nearby without a plant to record changes in the volume of water due to variation in temperature during the

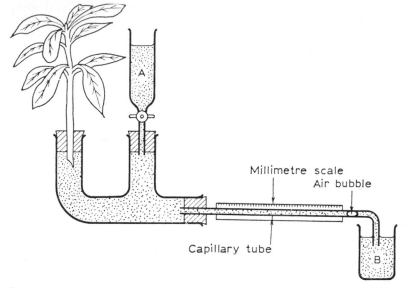

Fig. 5–2 Ganong potometer. A small air-bubble is introduced into the capillary tube by lifting it temporarily out of the water in B. When necessary the bubble can be moved back to the right-hand end of the tube by admitting water from the funnel.

experiment. It is important that the water should be at ambient temperature before the measurements begin.

The rate of water uptake by a cut shoot in a potometer is not necessarily the same as that of the shoot when attached to the plant because any water tensions in the xylem and the resistance of the root system to water movement are eliminated by cutting. Air may be introduced into some of the xylem vessels during excision, rendering them non-functional and thus increasing the overall resistance of the stem. For these reasons it is desirable where possible to use intact plants. Such experiments cannot be prolonged because of the difficulty of providing adequate aeration for the roots.

There is rarely an exact correlation between transpiration and absorption and especially with whole plants there is often an appreciable lag between a change in transpiration rate and a corresponding change in the rate of absorption (see Fig. 1–2, p. 3). Cut shoots attached to a potometer generally transpire more quickly than they absorb water and so they dry out gradually.

Water loss and absorption can be measured in the same experiment by a combination of the weighing and potometer methods. The plant is fixed in a potometer which is weighed at appropriate intervals; between weighings, measurements of water absorption are made by observing movement of an air bubble in the capillary tube.

5.1.7   Presentation of results

The amount of water transpired in a given time may be expressed on a per plant or per leaf basis, or alternatively per unit of leaf fresh weight, dry weight or area. Leaf areas can be measured by means of a planimeter; by counting the number of unit squares within the leaf outline traced on graph paper; or by cutting out the leaf outline drawn on paper and comparing the weight with that of a standard piece of the same paper of known area. Photometric instruments for the measurement of leaf area are now obtainable commercially. None of these methods is very convenient if the leaves remain attached to the plant. When it is desired to measure the area of attached leaves at intervals during an experiment, a photographic method of recording leaf area is best. Various types of photo-sensitive paper, suitable for this purpose, are available.

It is sometimes useful to compare the rates of transpiration expressed on a unit of surface area basis with evaporation from an atmometer* or evaporation pan placed under the same conditions. The ratio of the two rates (transpiration/evaporation) was termed relative transpiration by LIVINGSTON (1906) and BRIGGS and SHANTZ (1916). Variation in the value of the coefficient is an indication of the extent to which transpiration is affected by factors other than those controlling evaporation, i.e. the degree of control exerted by the plant.

5.2   Measurement of evapo-transpiration from plant communities

Agriculturalists, foresters and ecologists are often more interested in the total amount of water lost by a stand of vegetation in a given time, including evaporation from the soil than in absolute rates of transpiration. Approximate estimates of such evapo-transpiration can be made from the difference between precipitation and run-off of water from a given area over a period of time. On a sloping site where the sub-soil is impervious run-off can be estimated from the volume of water flowing in streams draining the area, while precipitation is measured by rain gauges. A more accurate method involves the use of a lysimeter in which the drainage water from a given area can be collected and measured. In one type of lysimeter the soil is enclosed in a concrete tank having an open top and perforated bottom from which drains run to a collecting vessel. The lysimeter must hold sufficient soil for normal development of the roots of a crop planted in it. The amount of water

* An atmometer is an instrument for measuring the rate of evaporation from a porous surface, e.g. filter paper or porous porcelain kept saturated with water. A standard evaporation pan approved by the World Meteorological Organisation is 122 cm in diameter and contains water to a depth of 25 cm.

supplied to the lysimeter, either artificially or as rain, is measured and compared with the quantity collected from it over a given time. Generally, it is assumed that the water contents of the soil and the plants growing in it are the same at the end of the experimental period as at the beginning. Some lysimeters have devices to maintain soil moisture at a constant level, while others can be weighed to determine how much water the soil has gained or lost.

Under conditions in which loss of water by drainage is negligible evapo-transpiration can be estimated by measuring changes in soil moisture content, e.g. with the help of a tensiometer. One type of tensiometer consists of a water-filled porous ceramic cup which is buried in the soil and connected by water-filled tubing to a manometer or pressure gauge, which can be calibrated to indicate water potential (see RICHARDS, 1949, for details). An alternative design employs a small block of gypsum, or similar porous material, which is placed in the soil. It is connected to a resistance bridge which enables conductivity to be measured. The water in the block reaches equilibrium with the soil water and its electrical resistance can be related to soil water content. Instead of estimating water loss over a period of time from the soil in a lysimeter, water can be added at intervals to keep soil moisture content at a fixed level. Evapo-transpiration can then be equated with the amount of water supplied over the experimental period.

An elegant method that has been employed successfully in estimating evapo-transpiration from forests is to measure the humidity of the air and wind-speed at several heights above the ground. From a knowledge of the physics of evaporation it is then possible to calculate the rate of evolution of water vapour from the vegetation.

When water is lost by evapo-transpiration it becomes vaporized and thus requires energy (see p. 14). The main source of this energy is solar radiation and in England about 40% of the incident energy is available for evaporation. The rest is either reflected or used in photosynthesis and in heating up the soil, air and plants. The amount of energy available sets a maximum value for the rate of evapo-transpiration provided that no other factor is limiting. This maximum is called potential evapo-transpiration and PENMAN (1948) devised an empirical formula whereby it can be calculated from meteorological data. MONTEITH (1965) has calculated that in the Thames Valley in Southern England potential evapo-transpiration is about 47 cm per year for short grass compared with 58 cm per year for taller crops such as wheat. Such estimates agree very well with the measured consumption of water by agricultural crops in Southern England, suggesting that when sufficient water is provided and the air relatively dry transpiration is controlled largely by the available energy.

5.3   Effect of environmental factors on transpiration

5.3.1   Light

The rate of transpiration characteristically exhibits a diurnal periodicity which is closely correlated with the movement of the stomata (see Chapter 4). In general, transpiration is low at night when the stomata are closed, increases rapidly after sunrise to a maximum in the late morning or early afternoon, and then falls gradually to its night value (Fig. 1-2). Of the various meteorological factors which fluctuate diurnally solar radiation appears to be most closely correlated with transpiration rate (Fig. 5-3). This is mainly due to the sensitivity of the stomata to light and to the fact that solar radiation provides energy for evaporation. As light energy must be absorbed before it can be utilized the colour of the evaporating surface has a marked effect on water loss both from an atmometer and from a plant, being greater from a dark, light-absorbing, surface than from one with high reflectance. Light has a greater effect on transpiration than on evaporation, that is the transpiration coefficient is higher in the light than in the dark, and this is attributable to a reduction in the effective evaporating surfaces of leaves in the dark when the stomata are closed.

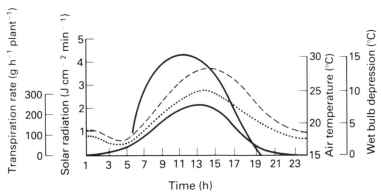

Fig. 5-3   Diurnal fluctuations in transpiration rate of oats (lower continuous line), solar radiation (upper continuous line), air temperature (dashed line) and humidity (dotted line). (Data from BRIGGS and SHANTZ, 1916.)

5.3.2   Humidity of the air

Transpiration occurs more rapidly when the air surrounding a plant is dry than when it is wet because the water potential gradient is larger (see below). Relative humidity is often used as a measure of the water content of the air because it is easy to measure, for example with wet and dry bulb thermometers. Relative humidity is the amount of water present in a given volume of air expressed as a percentage of the amount that the air can hold at the same temperature. However, for a given relative humidity value the water potential difference increases with increasing temperature and so a simple correlation between transpiration rate and relative humidity can be expected only at a particular temperature.

5.3.3 Temperature

If the absolute amount of water in the surrounding air remains constant an increase in temperature only has a small effect on water potential and therefore on transpiration. Nevertheless, when the temperature of the leaf is higher than that of the air the water potential gradient is higher than when the temperatures are the same, and in such circumstances a leaf can transpire even into water saturated air. On the other hand, leaves sometimes become cooler than the air and in this case dew may be deposited when the humidity is high.

The major effect of temperature on transpiration is through its effect on the condition of the stomata, either directly or by influencing CO_2 concentration (see Chapter 4).

5.3.4 Wind

Air movement over a leaf surface tends to remove water vapour and so increase the water potential gradient, thus promoting transpiration. However, at high wind-speeds, transpiration rate may fall because stomatal closure is induced, either by mechanical disturbance as a result of leaf shaking or by the increased water deficit leading to abscisic acid synthesis and subsequent stomatal closure.

5.3.5 Availability of water

If water supply to a plant is reduced, e.g. by drought or low temperature, absorption lags behind evaporation and the plant is placed under water stress. This causes the walls of the leaf cells to dry out and this reduces transpiration. When the water deficit becomes considerable the stomata close and this causes a further reduction in transpiration which may persist for several days even if water is subsequently supplied, presumably because ABA levels are maintained for a time after recovery.

5.4 Effects of plant structure on transpiration

Every plant species has a different rate of transpiration under a given set of environmental conditions and this is governed by the structure of its various parts. Of particular importance in this connection are surface area, shape and arrangement of leaves and their internal structure.

In general, plants having a large area of foliage transpire more rapidly on a per plant basis than those with a smaller leaf area, although per unit of leaf area the rate may be lower. This is because plants with a large leaf area tend to develop higher water deficits which reduce transpiration.

When a plant is pruned the rate of transpiration per unit area of the remaining leaves commonly increases for the same reason. Plants often shed their leaves when water stress becomes severe and reduction of leaf area is one of the characteristic features of xerophytes (see p. 9). The position and arrangement of leaves can affect transpiration because of mutual shading which influences the stomata and by effects on the pattern of air movement.

The leaves of different plant species and even those of the same leaf at different ages, may lose water at very different rates when expressed on a unit area basis. Such differences are attributable to structural features of the leaf and in particular to the structure and composition of the cuticle; the number, distribution, size and structure of stomata; the internal arrangement of cells and intercellular spaces, and location of vascular tissue. The contrasting features of leaves of a mesophyte (*Fagus sylvatica*) which loses water relatively quickly and of a xerophyte (*Pinus nigra*), which transpires slowly are shown in Fig. 5–4. Note particularly the thickened cuticle, epidermis and hypodermis, sunken stomata and lack of intercellular spaces in the leaf of *Pinus*. Leaves of a plant growing under different conditions, e.g. in sun or shade, also show differences in structure, e.g. thickness of cuticle, amount of spongy mesophyll and number or size of stomata, which affect water loss. The duration and extent of stomatal opening is also markedly affected by the conditions (see Chapter 4).

The properties of the cuticle influence transpiration profoundly, especially at night when the stomata are closed. In shade plants, such as ferns, where the cuticle is usually thin, as much as 30% of the total water

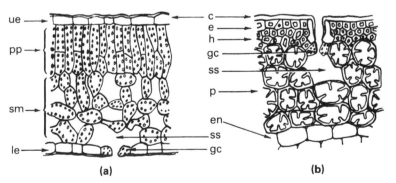

(a)   **(b)**

Fig. 5–4 Leaf structure. Transverse sections of (a) mesophytic leaf (beech, *Fagus sylvatica*) showing well-differentiated palisade parenchyma and spongy mesophyll; (b) xerophytic leaf (*Pinus nigra* showing thickened epidermis and hypodermis, sunken stomata and lack of intercellular spaces. c, cuticle; e, epidermis; ue, upper epidermis; le, lower epidermis; h, hypodermis; gc, guard cell; ss, sub-stomatal space; p, parenchyma; pp, palisade parenchyma; sm, spongy mesophyll; en, endodermis.

lost during the day is transpired through the cuticle (cuticular transpiration) whereas at night the amount may exceed 90%. In contrast, cuticular transpiration in some desert succulents is negligible (Table 12). Young leaves may have higher rates of cuticular transpiration than older leaves because the cuticle is thinner and less waxy, but in senescing leaves transpiration sometimes increases again because the cuticle cracks and becomes more porous.

Table 12   Cuticular transpiration of plants – several species under standard evaporative conditions. (From PISEK and BURGER, 1938.)

Species	Transpiration (mg h^{-1} g fresh weight of leaf^{-1})
Yellow balsam (*Impatiens noli-tangere*)	130.0
Marsh marigold (*Caltha palustris*)	47.0
Beech (*Fagus sylvatica*)	25.0
Oak (*Quercus robur*)	24.0
Stonecrop (*Sedum maximum*)	5.0
Scots pine (*Pinus sylvestris*)	1.5
Prickly pear (*Opuntia camanchica*)	0.1

The presence of hairs and scales on the surface of leaves might be expected to increase transpiration because of the increase in surface area. However, such structures often have an underlying layer of cuticle, and they tend to reduce transpiration rather than increase it by helping to retain moist air at the leaf surface. Another effect of hairs and scales is to make a leaf surface more reflective, and this cuts down transpiration by reducing the amount of solar radiation absorbed (see above). It also reduces the amount of heat that has to be dissipated (see SUTCLIFFE, 1977) and in view of this it is perhaps not surprising that many desert plants are densely hairy.

Plants which transpire rapidly tend to have more water-conducting elements in the leaves and stems than those which transpire slowly. In the extreme case of submerged aquatic angiosperms, vessels may be entirely lacking; xylem is also poorly developed in xerophytes. The relatively high resistance presented by the tracheid system in gymnosperms compared with the vessels of angiosperms (see Chapter 6) may be an important cause of the relatively low transpiration rates characteristic of these plants.

Some water is transpired from the surface of young stems but the amount of this on a unit of area basis is generally small compared with the amounts of water lost from leaves. This is attributable to the lower density of stomata and often the cuticular resistance is also higher. From older stems, water is lost mainly through the lenticels since the outer layers of the bark consist largely of cork cells in which the walls are impregnated with fat and therefore impermeable to water. Lenticular transpiration usually contributes only slightly to total transpiration but it accounts for most of the loss of water from deciduous trees after leaf fall.

5.5 Stomatal transpiration

Stomata were described in the seventeenth century by the Italian microscopist, Malpighi, who believed that they were involved in some way in the ventilation of a plant. It was not until the last century, however, that their role in the regulation of gas exchange between leaf and surrounding air was investigated. Following the observations of von Mohl and others that the size of stomata is controlled by light, it was generally accepted that CO_2 uptake and water loss from leaves occur mainly through these pores.

As long ago as 1961 it was shown that the amount of water lost from leaves may be as much as a third of that lost from a free water surface such as a piece of moist filter paper of the same area. As the area of open stomata is on average only about 1% of the total surface area of a leaf it is evident that water diffuses through stomata some thirty times more rapidly than from an equivalent free water surface. STEFAN (1881) showed that whereas the rate of evaporation from large bodies of water such as lakes is directly proportional to their area, the rate of diffusion from small circular areas is proportional to their perimeter, i.e. to linear dimensions, rather than to area. BROWN and ESCOMBE (1900) confirmed Stefan's deductions by measuring the rate of diffusion of CO_2 and water through perforated septa with varying numbers and size of holes, and later workers, e.g. SAYRE (1926), obtained similar results (Table 13).

The interpretation of this effect is that the points of equal water potential over an evaporating area form a series of oblate hemispheres and as a result the paths of diffusion of molecules along the water potential gradient are curved. Molecules diffusing from near the edge of the area escape more readily than those nearer the centre because the air is less saturated at a given distance from the pore near the edge than it is in the centre (Fig. 5–5a). The smaller the evaporating area the greater the proportion of molecules diffusing from near the edge and consequently

(a)   **(b)**

Fig. 5–5   Diffusion through small pores in still air. (a) Diffusion through a single pore. (b) Mutual interference between neighbouring pores. The arrowed lines show directions of diffusion and the dashed lines enclose areas of equal concentration of diffusing molecules. (After BANGE, 1953.)

Table 13   Relationship between the loss of water vapour through small openings in membranes and the area and perimeter of the pores. (From SAYRE, 1926.)

Diameter of pores (mm)	Loss of water (g)	Relative amounts of water lost	Relative areas of pores	Relative perimeter of pores
2.64	2.66	1.00	1.00	1.00
1.60	1.58	0.59	0.37	0.61
0.95	0.93	0.35	0.13	0.36
0.81	0.76	0.29	0.09	0.31
0.56	0.48	0.18	0.05	0.21
0.35	0.36	0.14	0.01	0.13

with decreasing size the rate of evaporation becomes more nearly proportional to linear dimensions than to area.

When a number of small evaporating surfaces are close enough together there is mutual interference between them and the rate of evaporation from each area is reduced and approaches that from a free water surface of the same area (Fig. 5–5b). VERDUN (1949) derived a mathematical expression for mutual interference between apertures in multi-perforate septa thus:

$$\log Q = \log Q_1 - \frac{k}{D^2}$$

where Q is the diffusion rate per pore; Q_1 the diffusion rate from an isolated pore; D the distance between pores; and k is a constant. Maximum values of Q were obtained for pores of different sizes at the following spacings:

> 0.8 mm – 20 pore diameters
> 0.4 mm – 30 pore diameters
> 0.2 mm – 40 pore diameters

Measurements of stomatal spacing in a variety of plants gave D values ranging from 5.3 – 15.7 diameters. Since the maximum diameter of open stomata is only about 0.04 mm, it is evident that mutual interference between stomata is high. As stomata close the spacing increases and interference is reduced. Furthermore, as a stoma closes its pore becomes more elliptical (see Fig. 4–2d, e) and in consequence the change in perimeter for a given reduction in area is less than it would be if the pore remained spherical. For both these reasons stomatal closure may be expected to exert less control of transpiration than might have been expected until the pores are nearly closed (see below).

5.6   Control of transpiration

The rate of diffusion of water from one point to another is proportional to the water potential gradient and the resistance of the intervening pathway (see p. 20). The total resistance to diffusion from the surface of cells within a leaf tissue into the outer air can be represented by a network of resistances as shown in Fig. 5–6. Assuming that the resistance

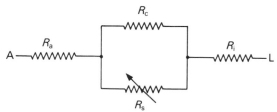

Fig. 5–6   Resistances encountered by a water molecule diffusing from a leaf cell (L) into the surrounding air (A). For explanation, see text.

of cuticle, R_c, is very high compared with that of the stomata, R_s, and that of the intercellular spaces, R_i, is relatively low, the transpirational flux i can be represented thus

$$i = \frac{\Delta \psi}{R_s + R_a}$$

where $\Delta \psi =$ the difference in water potential across the system and R_a is the resistance of the boundary layer of unstirred air at the leaf surface through which water molecules must diffuse.

The extent to which R_s controls transpiration depends on the relative values of R_s and R_a. In still air, R_a is relatively high and under these conditions R_s has relatively little influence except when the stomata are nearly closed and R_s correspondingly high. On the other hand, when air is moving over the surface of the leaf, R_a is much reduced and R_s has an effect over a wider range of stomatal aperture (Fig. 5–7).

Recognition that R_a may in some circumstances exert a predominant effect on transpiration rate helps to explain the significance of certain anatomical features associated with xerophytes. These plants often have small leaves with a dense covering of leaves or scales, a thick cuticle and sunken stomata. Despite this, when such plants are well supplied with water and the stomata open, they often lose as much or more water per unit area as do mesophytes. However, in comparison with mesophytes, wind has much less effect on the transpiration rate of xerophytes, presumably because hairs and sunken stomata help to maintain a layer of moist air in the vicinity of the stomata and so R_a remains high under these conditions.

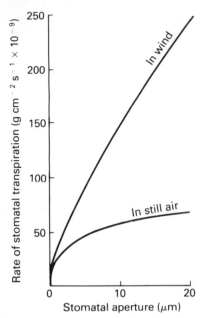

Fig. 5–7   Effect of the size of the stomatal aperture on the rate of stomatal transpiration in *Zebrina* in still air and in wind. (After BANGE, 1953.)

5.7   The significance of transpiration

Transpiration is the inevitable consequence of the fact that a plant must expose to the air a large area of moist cell walls in order to facilitate the absorption of CO_2 by the leaves. If plants had evolved a cuticle which allowed the free passage of CO_2 and oxygen, but not water, as do certain synthetic silicone rubber membranes that have recently been developed for use in hospital and diving equipment, they would presumably not transpire.

That transpiration is a necessary evil is indicated by the fact that it is reduced as much as possible when photosynthesis stops, and at times of water stress transpiration is cut down even at the expense of reduced photosynthesis and slower growth. In recent years, attempts have been made to find substances which when applied to plants will reduce transpiration without having a detrimental effect on growth. Among the substances that have been tried as anti-transpirants are silicone oils and low viscosity waxes applied as sprays with the object of forming a film permeable to CO_2 and oxygen, but not to water vapour. An alternative approach is to apply a substance such as abscisic acid or the fungicide phenylmercuric acetate at a concentration which causes partial closure of the stomata. Partial closure of stomata has a greater effect on the diffusion of water vapour out of a leaf than of carbon dioxide into it because whereas water has to diffuse only from the cell walls, CO_2 has to enter cells and penetrate into the chloroplasts. The extra resistance encountered makes R_i for CO_2 (see Fig. 5–6) much higher than for water and so altering R_s has a smaller effect on the rate of diffusion of CO_2 into the leaf than of water out of it. Nevertheless, all anti-transpirants reduce photosynthesis, and hence yield, to some extent, except under conditions of extreme drought. Their use depends on the reduction in value of the yield being smaller than the saving in irrigation costs.

From time to time it has been claimed that transpiration has some beneficial effects on plant growth which serve to mitigate the problems it brings. It is possible that in some situations a plant may deplete the soil of inorganic nutrients, e.g. phosphate, in the immediate vicinity of its roots to such an extent that growth is affected. A rapid rate of movement of soil water into a plant as a result of transpiration helps to prevent this by bringing dissolved substances to the root surface from more distant regions of the soil. There is some evidence that this effect may sometimes be important in improving the uptake of fertilizers by agricultural crops.

At one time it was believed that mineral salts were absorbed passively by roots and carried into the shoot via the transpiration stream. It now appears (see SUTCLIFFE and BAKER, 1974) that the absorption of water and dissolved substances are largely independent processes and that once mineral salts enter the root adequate supplies are distributed throughout the plant even at low transpiration rates.

Leaves exposed to solar radiation absorb a large amount of energy and consequently the leaf tends to get hot. Sometimes, heating is so severe that photosynthesis is inhibited for a time until the leaf cools down again. Because of the latent heat of evaporation transpiration has a powerful cooling effect and although this may not be of great significance in temperate regions, it is an important factor in the regulation of leaf temperature in hot desert environments (see SUTCLIFFE, 1977).

6 Movement of Water through Plants

6.1 Pathways of water movement

Being a plant physiologist I am often asked how water gets to the top of tall trees, and sometimes it is suggested to me that no one really knows the answer. In fact, water flows through plants along a gradient of water potential existing between the soil solution and surrounding air. Despite its structural complexity, the part played by a plant in the transport of water from soil to air is not basically different from that of a pipe through which water is lifted by a pump. The main motive force is located outside the plant and not within it, although, as we have seen (Chapter 3), osmotic forces are responsible for the accumulation of water in cells.

The water in plants can be divided into three distinct fractions in which water is moving at different rates and sometimes in different directions. These fractions are:

(i) Water present in the spaces within the cell walls and in the water film surrounding them, which together comprise the apoplasm. Water-filled cavities in dead cells, such as those of the xylem, are included in the apoplasm, and it is through them that long distance movement of water mainly occurs.

(ii) Water in the protoplasts of invididual cells which are continuous with one another via plasmodesmata, forming the symplasm. The water in sieve tubes in the phloem is considered to be part of this fraction.

(iii) Water occurring in the vacuoles of living cells.

Water is transported from one place to another within the plant along water potential gradients caused, for example, by evaporation from leaf cells, growth, or by local accumulation of solutes. The water in vacuoles, and to some extent in the xylem, should be looked upon as a reserve supply which is drawn upon in times of water stress and replenished when water is available. As was mentioned earlier (p. 3), plants commonly lose more water through transpiration during the day than they absorb by the roots, and make up the deficit at night (Fig. 1-2). It was also pointed out that the water content of deciduous trees often falls progressively while they are in leaf and increases again after leaf fall. Although some water is removed from the vacuoles of living cells in the trunk during periods of high transpiration, much of it comes from the cavities of dead xylem elements and cell walls, which tend to dry out.

Long-distance movement of water in plants from roots to leaves which occurs predominantly in the xylem is referred to as the transpiration stream. Movement occurs in response to a water potential gradient between the evaporating surfaces and the soil solution, caused mainly by transpiration but it is augmented by root pressure resulting from solute accumulation in the xylem of the root (see below).

A relatively small amount of water may be transported for long distances through the phloem and the driving forces involved are still uncertain. It is likely that water potential gradients created by the accumulation of solutes, especially sucrose, in the sieve tube sap in one place, e.g. of a leaf, and their removal elsewhere is responsible for some transport of water in the phloem but other mechanisms such as electro-osmosis (see p. 27), peristaltic pumping and cytoplasmic streaming have also been invoked (RICHARDSON, 1975).

Such transport of water as occurs in the phloem is often, but not always, in the opposite direction to that taking place in the xylem, leading to a circulation of water in the plant. The water supply to organs such as fruits and potato tubers which do not transpire very rapidly is probably mainly through the phloem. Even less is known about the transport of water through the unspecialized cytoplasm of parenchyma cells, e.g. in the root cortex and leaf mesophyll, than about phloem transport. It appears that the resistance to such movement is high judging by the large hydrostatic pressures that are required to draw water through the cytoplasm of cortical cells in excised root systems (MEES and WEATHERLEY, 1957). It is unlikely that much water moves from cell vacuole to vacuole across the root cortex in response to a water potential gradient in the way that some authors have suggested (see for example Fig. 12–5 in Roberts, 1976). This is because of the very high resistance of this pathway even compared with the symplastic route involving as it does transport across the plasmalemma, tonoplast and intervening cytoplasm twice for each cell that is traversed.

The movement of water from soil in the transpiration stream through a plant and into the surrounding air can be compared with an electrical circuit consisting of resistances and capacitors (Fig. 6–1). The rate of movement through each part of this catenary system depends on the water potential gradient and on the resistance. The capacitors represent the ability of plant tissues to store water and release it according to the prevailing conditions. The largest resistance and the largest potential difference occurs in the gaseous phase between the evaporating surfaces of the leaf cells and the surrounding air. Stomata have an important influence on this resistance and so exert major control on water movement through the whole system. Changes of resistance, for example of the xylem, have a much smaller effect unless there is severe disruption of the conducting elements (see below), and the stomata are open. The resistance of the root system is usually of minor importance but if the continuity between water in the root apoplasm and in the surrounding soil is broken the resistance at the interface increases enormously. This is why transplanting large plants often leads to temporary wilting.

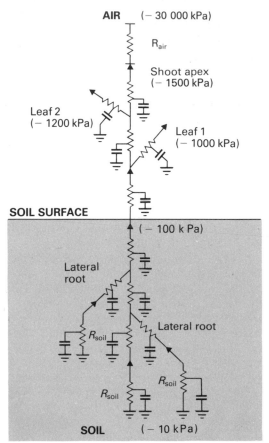

Fig. 6–1 Pathway of water movement from soil to air through a plant, showing resistances encountered in soil (R_{soil}), root, stem, leaf and air (R_{air}). The capacitors represent the storage capacities of soil and plant parts. Figures show hypothetical fall in water potential in various parts of the system.

Both an increase in the water potential of the air as a result of increased humidity and a fall in that of the soil as it becomes dry decreases the water potential gradient and reduce water movement through the system as a whole. But whereas the first treatment decreases water stress the latter increases it causing depletion of water reserves within the plant.

6.2 Transport of water in the xylem

6.2.1 Structure of xylem

In ferns, gymnosperms and angiosperms long distance transport of water occurs mainly through the dead remains of specialized cells in the xylem, In ferns and gymnosperms the xylem, or wood, is composed largely of spindle-shaped cells or tracheids, orientated with their long axes parallel to that of the stem. They overlap one another and have thick lignified walls. In gymnosperms the walls of the tracheids are perforated by large characteristically shaped pores – the so-called bordered pits (Figs 6–2a and 6–3b). The tracheids, which lose their living contents after cell wall growth is complete are interspersed with living parenchyma cells, also with lignified walls. These cells are arranged in sheets or 'rays' running radially across the stem which serve to maintain cytoplasmic continuity between the bark and the living cells in the centre of the stem and are not involved in longitudinal water transport. The xylem of most angiosperms is more complicated than that of gymnosperms in that the xylem includes, besides tracheids and parenchyma, some thick-walled elongated fibres which serve to strengthen the tissue and vessels which are the important water-conducting elements (Fig. 6–3a). Vessels are formed from a longitudinal file of cells (vessel segments) in which the connecting walls disappear during development to form open tubes. Sometimes, as in 'ring-porous' trees, such as the ash (*Fraxinus excelsior*), the vessels may be several metres long. Pits, which are usually elliptical and more numerous than in gymnosperms, occur on the walls of adjoining vessels making the cavities of the tubes continuous with one another (Fig. 6–2b). There are no vessels in some angiosperm genera (e.g. *Drimys*) and in contrast, vessels have been found in a few pteridophytes, e.g. bracken (*Pteridium aquilinum*), but in no gymnosperms. For further details of the structure of wood see GEMMELL (1969).

The presence of living cells in the stem is, of course, indirectly necessary for water movement insofar as the conducting elements often function for a relatively short time (see below) and their continuous replacement depends on the activity of living cambial cells adjoining them.

6.2.2   *Velocity of flow*

The quantity of water (Q) transported through a stem in unit time can be calculated from the formula $Q = Av$ where A is the cross-sectional area of the cavities through which transport occurs and v is the linear velocity.

Q can be estimated from measurements of transpiration (see Chapter 5) and if v is known the cross-section area of the functional channels may be calculated. SACHS (1887) attempted to measure v by observing the rate of transport of lithium ions through the stems of intact plants after lithium nitrate had been applied to the roots. More recently, fluorescent dyes and radioactive substances have been used in a similar way. In one of the earliest experiments involving the application of a radioactive isotope to plants, ARNON, STOUT and SIPOS (1940) found that radioactivity could be detected in the leaves of a rapidly transpiring tomato plant over a metre in length 40 minutes after supplying ^{32}P-labelled phosphate to the roots. Under conditions of low transpiration the time taken for the isotope to travel to the leaves was much longer.

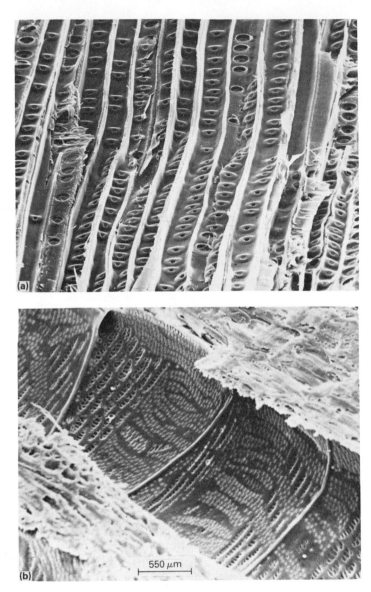

Fig. 6–2 The structure of xylem in seed plants. Scanning electron micrographs of (a) *Pinus strobus* (white pine) showing tracheids with numerous borded pits seen in surface view on radial walls. (b) *Quercus alba* (oak) showing a large vessel in surface view. Note vessel segments and numerous pits. (Photographs by courtesy of Dr M. C. Ledbetter, Biology Department, Brookhaven, National Laboratory, Long Island, U.S.A.)

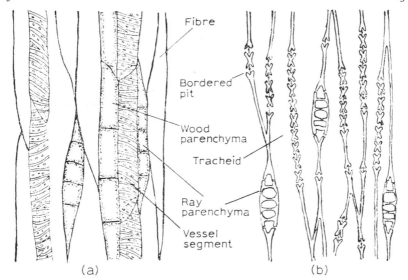

Fibre

Bordered
pit

Wood
parenchyma

Tracheid

Ray
parenchyma

Vessel
segment

(a)   (b)

Fig. 6–3   Structure of xylem in: (a) an angiosperm (*Tilia*), and (b) a gymnosperm
(*Pinus*) as seen in longitudinal section.

When the rate of flow of the transpiration stream is measured by
determining the rate of movement of a solute it is assumed that the water
and solute are moving at the same rate. To confirm this it is necessary to
measure the rate of transport of water itself. This can be done by injecting
tritium-labelled water into the xylem and comparing its rate of
movement with that of an ion such as ^{32}P-labelled phosphate.

6.2.3   Evidence that water is transported in the xylem

Circumstantial evidence that the xylem is the tissue mainly involved in
the transport of water from roots to leaves of plants comes from the
observation that there is a correlation between transpiration rates and the
amount of xylem supplying a particular leaf. There is very little xylem in
the veins of the submerged leaves of water plants whereas those of
emergent leaves contain a large number of vessels and tracheids. The
leaves of mesophytes which transpire relatively rapidly have vascular
bundles typically with much more xylem than is usually found in
xerophytes.

More direct evidence that the xylem is the tissue responsible for water
movement through stems comes from 'ringing' or girdling experiments.
If a complete section of bark is removed from a woody stem, leaving the
xylem intact the leaves above the ring remain turgid, whereas if a section
of xylem is removed the leaves wilt rapidly. In some cases interruption of
the xylem on one side of the stem prevents water moving into leaves
situated vertically above the cut, but leaves inserted elsewhere remain

turgid indicating that in these plants there is very little lateral transfer in the xylem. In other cases some lateral transport occurs (see section 6.3 below).

Ringing experiments do not show through which cells in the xylem water actually moves. Because vessels are open tubes running for long distances without interruption, it seems obvious that they must be the main channels for the transpiration stream when they occur. Support for this assertion comes from experiments on the uptake of dyes and radioactive tracers. When a stem is cut under an aqueous solution of a dye, such as eosin, the liquid is taken in, and except near the cut surface where there is general staining of cells, only the walls of the xylem vessels and tracheids above the cut are coloured. This shows that, at least in cut stems, the vessels and tracheids offer the path of least resistance to flow of aqueous solutions and that movement occurs in them predominantly towards a transpiring organ. Reduction in transpiration rate causes a considerable increase in the length of time required for the dye to reach the veins of a leaf. Experiments with intact seedlings, with their roots immersed in solutions of dye have given similar results. Near the root tips, the meristem and cortical cells become uniformly coloured, but within the stele staining is seen mainly in the walls of the tracheids and vessels.

Instead of using dyes, radioactive substances, e.g. sodium phosphate labelled with ^{32}P, may be added as tracers to the water, and their location determined subsequently by autoradiography. These experiments, like those with dyes are open to the criticism that water does not necessarily travel in the stem along the same pathway as dissolved substances. This objection can be overcome by the use of tritium labelled water (see below).

SACHS (1887), thought that water is transported in the stems of plants by capillarity in the walls of the vessels and tracheids rather than through the cell cavities, which he suggested might be filled with air. Although water can rise to considerable heights by capillarity in narrow spaces, such as those that occur in cell walls, the resistance offered by such channels is much too high to allow flow of the transpiration stream at the rates observed. It has been shown experimentally that when the cavities of xylem vessels are occluded by immersing a cut stem for a short time in molten paraffin wax, which does not penetrate into the cell wall spaces, the leaves wilt even when the stem is subsequently transferred to water. Further evidence against Sach's proposal is that in plants with flexible stems, such as vines, the transpiration stream can be stopped by squeezing the stem sufficiently to close the xylem cavities.

6.2.4 Evidence that xylem transport is passive

The fact that water apparently moves up a stem through dead xylem elements implies it is a passive process and that living cells in the stem are not directly involved. The best evidence supporting this comes from an experiment, first performed by STRASBURGER (1891), which shows that after the living cells adjoining the xylem have been killed by poison a stem still conducts water. He cut across the base of a young oak tree and immersed the cut end in a barrel of picric acid. After allowing time for the transport of the poison into the leaves he replaced the solution by water containing a dye. Subsequent observation showed that the dye ascended quickly into the leaves. More recently, it has been shown that injection of metabolic inhibitors into xylem vessels of intact plants does not interfere with upward transport of water (KURTZMANN, 1966).

If a section of a stem is killed by heat or by application of metabolic poisons it is often observed that the leaves above the treated region eventually wilt. DIXON (1914) argued that this is an indirect effect resulting from blocking of the conducting elements by substances derived from the dead cells. HANDLEY (1939) observed that application of low temperatures to a section of stem of an intact plant causes it to wilt. He attributed this to interference with metabolism of cells adjoining the xylem, but more recently, ZIMMERMANN (1965) has shown that water movement is affected only if the applied temperature is low enough to cause the xylem sap to freeze.

An ingenious thermo-electric method, originally used to measure the rate of circulation of blood, was developed by HUBER and SCHMIDT (1937) to estimate the rate of flow of the transpiration stream in trees. The method involves brief application of heat to a localized region of the stem, and measurement by means of sensitive thermocouples of the rate of its subsequent transfer upwards and downwards from the point of application. From the difference in the time taken for the heat to be transferred in the two directions the rate of movement of the transpiration stream in the surface layer of xylem can be calculated. Rates varying from near zero to over 100 cm per hour were recorded depending on the time of day at which the observations were made (Fig. 6–4). Huber and Schmidt found that there was a gradual lowering in velocity from the base to the apex of trees. This was attributed to an increase in the effective cross-sectional area of conducting xylem in the upper parts of the plants.

A study of the relationship between the amounts of water loss by a plant and the rates of linear flow indicate that in ring-porous trees, movement of water longitudinally is mainly in the outermost annual ring. The large vessels which carry most of the water seem to function only during the season in which they are formed, becoming filled with air before leaf fall and being replaced by new water-filled vessels associated with a new crop of leaves in the next season. In diffuse porous trees the individual vessels appear to carry water for several years, while in conifers a tracheid functions for even longer.

It appears that in most trees there is much more xylem than is actually needed to supply the leaves with water. This is shown by the fact that if

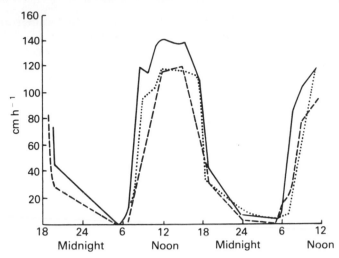

Fig. 6–4 Diurnal variation in the rate of sap movement in *Larix* (——), *Picea* (– – – – –) and *Fagus* (· · · · · ·). (HUBER and SCHMIDT, 1937.)

some of the xylem vessels or tracheids are severed by makiing a horizontal cut into the trunk transpiration from the leaves above is often hardly affected; the rate of flow of water through the remaining elements is simply increased. Even when two overlapping cuts are made (Fig. 6–5), the water supply to the upper parts is not necessarily cut off, provided that the two cuts are not too close together. This is because water can move laterally in the xylem through the pits in the cell walls and although the resistance to water in this direction is considerably greater than that of longitudinal flow in vessels, sufficient water may move via this pathway to prevent the leaves above from wilting. Eventually, through the activity of the cambium, new xylem elements develop forming vessels which take

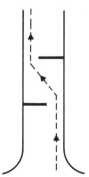

Fig. 6–5 Demonstration that water can move laterally through a tree trunk to circumvent two overlapping cuts. For explanation, see text.

a sinuous route round the cuts and thus the continuity of water columns in xylem vessels is restored. POSTLEWAITE and ROGERS (1958) showed that when a solution containing ^{32}P labelled phosphate is injected into the xylem on one side of a pine tree the isotope normally moves directly up the tree with little lateral displacement. However, if deep saw cuts are made in the trunk above the point of injection the isotope moves laterally round the cuts in the most recently-formed xylem.

6.3   Mechanism of water movement in the xylem

6.3.1   The tensile strength of water

In order to bring about the mass-flow of water upwards through the xylem force must be applied to overcome the influence of gravity and the resistance presented by the conducting channels. If a tube is filled with water and sealed at one end and then stood upright with the open end downwards dipping below a free water surface, there will be a pressure gradient down the tube from zero at the top to nearly atmospheric pressure at the bottom. This gradient is due to the weight of water in the column, i.e. it is caused by gravity, and amounts to about 10 kPa per metre of column. Atmospheric pressure is thus insufficient to support a water column of more than about 10 m, but if the open end of the tube is dipped into water in a closed container to which additional pressure might be applied the height of the column could be increased up to limits set by the cohesive forces between water molecules and the adhesive forces between the water and walls of the tube (see Chapter 2). The tensile strength of water is very high and FISHER (1948) estimated that theoretically a tension of some 130 000 kPa is necessary to break a stretched water column. Experimentally determined values for water and expressed xylem sap are much lower than this, ranging from about 2500 kPa to over 30 000 kPa depending on the method of measurement. Determinations of the tensile strength of water have most often been made by Berthelot's 'water hammer'. This involves filling a tube with water and sealing it to leave a small bubble of water saturated air inside. The liquid is expanded by raising the temperature until it completely fills the tube and is then allowed to cool until the bubble reappears. The tension developed in the water before cavitation can be calculated from the change in volume of the liquid and its coefficient of expansion.

6.3.2   Capillarity

If an open-ended tube is placed vertically with one end immersed in water, the liquid will rise in the tube until the weight of the water column balances the attractive forces operating between the water and the walls of the tube. The narrower the tube the higher the liquid will rise because the surface-active forces are greater relative to the force of gravity. In a glass tube of 0.01 mm bore water will rise by capillarity to a height of about three metres; the rise in a plastic tube of the same bore is much smaller because of the lower surface tension. On the other hand, water will rise by capillarity to greater heights in xylem vessels than in glass tubes of the same diameter because of the very high attractive forces between water and the cell walls. SACHS (1887) pointed out that water could rise by capillarity to the top of tall trees if it moved in the narrow spaces between the cellulose fibres in cell walls, as in a wick. Whilst this may be true experiments have shown that the resistance of cell wall to water movement is so high that this cannot be a major pathway for the transpiration stream (see p. 90). Even to overcome the resistance offered by xylem vessels in an ash tree to water flow through the lumina at the rates observed, a pressure gradient of about 15 kPa per metre is required (ZIMMERMAN, 1965). It has been suggested that there may be a gradient of matric potential in the xylem (see p. 102) caused by the presence of gel-like material lining the cell walls and if the amount of this material increases with height it could have a significant role in the upward movement of water, especially at low transpiration rates.

6.3.3   *The cohesion-tension theory*

The close relationship between transpiration and the rate of movement of water in stems suggests that evaporation is involved in the regulation of water movement in the xylem. One way in which this might occur is illustrated by the physical model illustrated in Fig. 6–6. As water evaporates from the porous surface, capillary forces maintain the position of water menisci in the pores causing reduced pressure inside the pot. A pressure gradient is thus created which causes water to flow through the tube and water may rise in such a system to heights in excess of that achieved by atmospheric pressure ($\simeq 10$ metres $= 760$ mm of mercury).

BOEHM (1892) showed that the same thing may happen when the porous pot is replaced by a transpiring shoot and he suggested that water moves into the leaves of plants in a similar way as a result of transpiration. This idea was elaborated by DIXON (1914) in his classic monograph on *Transpiration and the Ascent of Sap* and is commonly known as the cohesion theory. Although it has not been conclusively proved and is still a matter of some controversy (see e.g. PLUMB and BRIDGMAN, 1972, 1973), the proposal is sufficiently well established to justify calling it a theory, rather than a hypothesis.

According to the cohesion theory a decrease in water potential at the sites of evaporation in the cell walls of a leaf causes a bulk flow of water through the apoplasm from the xylem terminals which are rarely situated more than one or two cells from an evaporating surface. Some water undoubtedly flows from the xylem to the evaporating surfaces in the symplasm but as the resistance of the symplastic pathway is considerably greater than the apoplastic pathway relatively little water moves along this

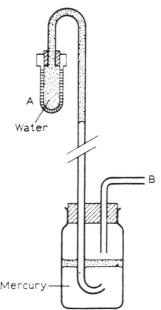

Fig. 6–6 The cohesion theory. A demonstration that evaporation can raise water to a height greater than is possible by atmospheric pressure. It is essential that the water in the porous pot, A, and connecting tube is free of air. This can be accomplished by surrounding A with a beaker of boiling water, and allowing excess water and air to escape from B. When the beaker is removed evaporation from A causes the level of mercury in the tube to rise to a height which may exceed 76 cm.

route. Water in the cytoplasm and vacuoles of leaf cells tends to equilibrate with water in the apoplasm (see Chapter 3) and the water potential of leaf cells is an indication of the force developed through evaporation. When transpiration rates are high a leaf is less turgid and its water potential is lower than when transpiration is low.

As a result of withdrawal of water from the xylem the sap is placed under tension which is transmitted downwards through the continuous water columns existing in vessels and tracheids from leaves down to the roots. The reduced water potential in the xylem sap will cause water to move towards the conducting elements from the soil solution via the cortex and endodermis. As in the case of the leaf, movement of water across the cortex in response to transpiration is mainly through the apoplasm, but movement through the endodermis is restricted to the symplasm because the apoplasmic pathway is blocked by the Casparian bands (see Fig. 6–7).

The existence of water under tension in the xylem is indicated by the fact that the diameter of a stem is often reduced at high transpiration rates as might be expected if the conducting elements contract when the

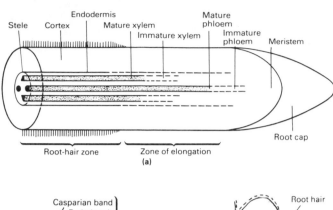

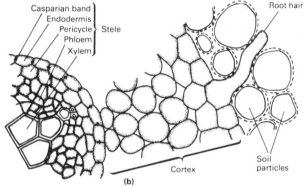

Fig. 6–7 Root structure. (a) Root tip showing various zones, and the regions of differentiation of xylem and phloem. (b) Transverse section of a root in the root hair zone.

contents are under tension. MACDOUGAL (1925) devised a sensitive measuring device or 'dendrograph' and observed that the diameter of tree trunks decreases during the day as water stress develops reaching a minimum value in the afternoon after which the trunk swells again to a maximum diameter in the early morning. The stems of herbaceous plants show similar diurnal changes in diameter but in this case changes in the volume of living cells of the cortex and pith as water stress increases and decreases are largely responsible for the effect. The relative rigidity of the walls of xylem elements compared with those of non-lignified cells means that they change in volume relatively little for a given change in water potential (see Chapter 3).

Another indication that the xylem sap in transpiring plants is under reduced pressure is the observation that when a xylem vessel is exposed by removing a segment of bark and then injected with a solution of dye, the liquid travels very rapidly at first both upwards and downwards as the tension is relieved (PRESTON, 1958). By use of the pressure bomb technique

(p. 41), SCHOLANDER *et al.* (1965) were able to show that hydrostatic pressures ranging from −4000 kPa in forest trees in moist soil to −8000 kPa in desert shrubs, occur in xylem sap. They also confirmed that water potential of xylem sap becomes increasingly negative with increasing height above the ground.

Thus it seems likely that one of the basic requirements of the cohesion theory, namely, the existence of tensions in the xylem sap of transpiring plants is met. Criticism of the cohesion theory nowadays rests mainly on two points.

(i) The possibility that the pressure gradient developed as a result of evaporation is insufficient to move water through the xylem at the observed rates.

(ii) The requirement that continuous columns of water must exist between the evaporating surfaces and water in the free space of the root.

With regard to the first point, it has been shown that a 10 m log of a conifer requires a pressure of about 150 kPa to drive water through it at a rate comparable to the normal flow of xylem sap. Therefore, a pressure gradient of 1500 kPa should be sufficient to move water at the rates observed to the tops of the tallest conifers, the giant redwoods, the tallest of which are about 100 m high. The force required to drive water through the trunks of birch and maple trees at the higher rates observed in these angiosperms is about double that for conifers, but even if this is characteristic of deciduous trees generally, 3000 kPa should be sufficient to move water to the tops of the tallest of these trees, the Blue Gums (*Eucalyptus* spp.) of Australia which also grow to about 100 m. Leaf water potentials of −3000 to −4000 kPa are not uncommon in such trees. It is said that the highest branches of the tallest trees in the world have stopped growing and perhaps this is because the water potentials developed are only just sufficient to raise water to the uppermost leaves. It may be significant that there is a tendency for tree leaves to have lower (i.e. more negative) water potentials, than shrubs and herbaceous plants and that leaves near the tops of trees have the lowest water potentials of all. It seems to me that there is likely to be an adequate water potential gradient even in the tallest trees to account for the flow of water at the rates observed.

Much of the criticism of the cohesion theory in the past has rested on doubt about the continuity of water columns in the xylem. Experiments with long water columns in capillary tubes indicate that despite their high tensile strength the water columns are extremely delicate when placed under tension and liable to fracture on slight mechanical disturbance. It is argued that the water columns in xylem vessels would similarly be very labile and break, for example when the branches sway in the wind. There is no doubt that the water columns in the xylem of plants do break sometimes and the conducting elements become filled with air and water vapour. When cavitation occurs the receding water columns produce vibrations which can be heard as 'clicks' with the aid of a sensitive microphone and amplifier (MILBURN, 1973). However, presence of air in even a high percentage of the conducting channels does not invalidate the cohesion theory, since only a small number of elements need to be functional at any time to supply the needs of the plant (see p. 91). In cases where plant stems are transparent enough it is possible to see that at least some of the vessels are filled with water even under conditions of severe wilting. Presumably a sufficient number of new xylem elements become functional during each growing season to replace those that become filled with air. The experiment in which overlapping cuts are made (Fig. 6–5) which must break all the vertical water columns at some point, shows that · leaves may continue to receive some water by lateral transfer from one vertical channel to another until the continuity of vessels is restored. It must also be remembered that the water columns in xylem vessels are not isolated from one another as in glass tubes, but are linked laterally via the pores forming a three dimensional continuum which may well make the plant system more stable than experiments with model systems suggest.

It is well known that the density of the wood in the trunks of deciduous trees decreases during the growing season because of the replacement of some water by air (see Chapter 1, p. 3). After leaf fall when transpiration rates are lower the xylem refills with water forced into it from below by root pressure (see below).

6.4 Availability of soil water

Soil is a heterogeneous medium consisting of solid, liquid and gaseous phases. Water occurs in soil in each of these phases: it is present as water of hydration in the solid phase, as free and bound water in the liquid phase and as water vapour. Water associated with the solid phase, sometimes referred to as 'imbibed' water, is not easily removed from soil because of the high matric forces by which it is retained and is mainly unavailable to plants. Water vapour which is present in the air spaces between soil particles is readily absorbed by roots, but is quantitatively a minor source of water to most plants.

Plants obtain the bulk of their water from the liquid phase in which two fractions are distinguished.

(i) *Gravitational water* which temporarily displaces air from spaces between soil particles following rain and gradually percolates downwards under the influence of gravity. If gravitational water remains indefinitely, the soil is said to be waterlogged and it is then unsuitable for growth of most plants because of lack of aeration. However marsh and bog plants and a few crop species notably rice (*Orzya sativa*) and taro (*Colocasia esculentum*) grow well under these conditions.

(ii)   *Capillary water* comprises the bulk of the water remaining in the soil after gravitational water has drained away and it is the main source of supply for most plants. The water is held as thin films near the surface of soil particles and in the small capillary spaces between them. Soil containing the maximum amount of capillary water but no gravitational water is said to be at its field capacity. Field capacity, which is usually expressed in terms of water content as a percentage of dry weight, is lower for a clay soil, in which the solid particles are relatively small than for a sandy soil in which the particles are much larger (Fig. 6–8).

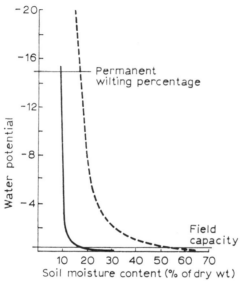

Fig. 6–8   Relationship between water potential (kPa×10^{-2}) and moisture content in a sandy soil (——) and a clay soil (– – – –). (After KRAMER, 1969.)

The permanent wilting percentage (PWP) is the water content of a soil (again expressed as a percentage of the dry weight) at which the leaves of a test plant growing in it under standard conditions of light intensity, temperature, humidity, etc., becomes wilted and remains so until additional water is added. Using the water potential terminology the PWP is reached when ψ_{soil} is equal to ψ_{plant}, and so the plant cannot absorb any more water from the soil until ψ_{soil} is raised. A wide range of crop plants has been found to reduce the water content of the soil to about the same level before permanent wilting occurs and −1500 kPa is commonly equated in agricultural practice with PWP (Fig. 6–8). Xerophytes can reduce the water potential of soil to much lower levels than this while some halophytes can absorb water from saline soils in which ψ_{soil} may be as low as −20 000 kPa.

Total soil-moisture stress (TSMS) is a term introduced by WADLEIGH and AYERS (1945). To indicate the water potential of a soil, TSMS or ψ_{soil} can be conveniently divided into a number of components thus:

$$\psi_{soil} = \psi_\pi + \psi_m + \psi_p + \psi_g$$

where

ψ_π = osmotic potential
ψ_m = matric potential
ψ_p = pressure potential
ψ_g = gravitational potential

$\psi_p \simeq 100$ kPa, ψ_g is negligible, and ψ_s is generally low (< 10 kPa) except in saline soils, so ψ_{soil} is mainly determined by ψ_m which decreases markedly as water contents falls from field capacity to PWP (Fig. 6–8).

The most accurate method of determining ψ_{soil} is to measure psychrometrically the water potential of the air above the soil sample enclosed in a container at constant temperature (p. 26). Techniques for determining ψ_{soil} in the field include the use of a thermistor hygrometer, a tensiometer, or a conductivity block (see p. 74).

6.5   Absorption of water by roots

Water is absorbed by roots from soil mainly in the region of the root hairs. The root hair zone is a particularly favourable one for absorption because it presents a large surface area in intimate contact with water films surrounding the soil particles (Fig. 6–7). Individual root hairs usually function for only a few days and are replaced progressively by others near the tip of the root as it grows. In this way the root hair zone is brought progressively into contact with new regions of the soil. In some trees, e.g. pines and beech, mycorrhizal fungi associated with the roots help to increase the surface area for absorption.

Plants grown in solution culture commonly lack root hairs as do the roots of aquatic plants. In these cases, water absorption takes place over the whole root surface, as indeed it does to some extent also in plants growing in soil. There appears to be an appreciable absorption of water through the suberized surfaces of older roots, e.g. in trees, and this is particularly important during dormant periods when young growing roots and root hairs may be lacking.

Water movement across the cortex towards the endodermis of a root (Fig. 6–7) occurs mainly in the apoplasm in response to a water potential gradient between the xylem sap permeating the free space of the stele and the soil solution. As long as the water potential of the xylem sap is more negative than that of the soil solution bulk flow of water will occur inwards through the cortical cell walls and surface films. A smaller amount of water (possibly only a few per cent of the total in a rapidly transpiring plant) moves through the symplasm which presents a much higher resistance (10–100 times than the apoplasm to the bulk flow of water. Because of the even higher resistance very little water moves across the cortex from cell vacuole to cell vacuole in response to a water potential gradient. Many students make the mistake of supposing that movement of water across the root cortex depends on the osmotic potential decreasing progressively inwards across the cortex. This is incorrect! There is no evidence that cells of the inner cortex have osmotic potentials that are significantly lower than that of the surface cells but they do have lower water potentials under normal conditions.

When water reaches the endodermis in the younger part of a root the apoplasmic pathway is blocked by the Casparian strips (Fig. 6–7), and further movement into the stele occurs via the symplasm and possibly through the vacuoles. The endodermis thus behaves as a semi-permeable membrane separating the xylem sap from the surrounding medium. Once inside the endodermis, water moves freely again in the apoplasm towards the xylem. When a decapitated root system is killed, e.g. by immersing in hot water, its resistance to the movement of water by suction applied to the cut end is drastically reduced. This is the result of membrane disruption which enables water to flow even more freely through cells than through the cell walls. Low temperature has the opposite effect presumably because the permeability of the cell membranes to water is reduced.

6.6   Root pressure and guttation

As has been indicated above, the water potential gradient between external solution and xylem sap of a transpiring plant is mainly due to the development of tension (negative ψ_p) in the xylem as a result of evaporation. Another contributory factor is the accumulation of solutes in the xylem sap which results in ψ_π being lower there than in the external solution. The actual value of ψ_π in the xylem sap depends not only on the intensity of solute transport but also on the rate of transpiration. The concentration of dissolved substances in xylem sap is low when a plant is transpiring rapidly and high when it is not (SUTCLIFFE and BAKER, 1974). Thus, whereas ψ_π contributes relatively little to the water potential of xylem sap in rapidly transpiring plants, it becomes important at low transpiration rates, leading to the development of a positive root pressure.

The osmotic potential of xylem sap falls to its lowest level in a de-shooted plant where transpiration is zero. If a manometer is connected to the stump of a potted plant such as a *Fuchsia* from which most of the shoot has been removed, the development of a positive pressure in the xylem sap by osmotic absorption of water can be demonstrated. Root pressure is very intense in certain plants under favourable conditions and notably so in vines. Stephen Hales reported in *Vegetable Staticks* (1727) that when he attached a ¼ inch (6 mm) diameter tube to a cut vine stem liquid rose in it to a height of over 21 feet (6.3 m) over a period of several days and he said '*would very probably have risen higher if the joynt had not leaked*'. He noticed that the level of the liquid rose much more quickly during the day than at night when sometimes it even fell. This diurnal periodicity in root pressure has been confirmed by later investigations and has sometimes been cited as evidence that metabolic processes are directly involved in water absorpition by roots (e.g. GROSSENBACHER, 1939). What actually happens is that there is a rhythm in the accumulation of solutes in the xylem sap as a result of fluctuating metabolic activity and this affects water absorption indirectly (ARISZ, HELDER and VAN DIE, 1951). As may be expected root pressure is reduced by lowering the temperature, by withholding inorganic nutrients and by metabolic inhibitors.

Sometimes positive pressures are developed in the xylem of intact plants and these are responsible for the phenomenon of 'guttation' – the release of liquid water from leaves. Guttation can be demonstrated readily by placing young seedlings (oat, barley and maize seedlings work very well) under a bell-jar in a warm laboratory. The liquid emerges either from stomata or from water pores (hydathodes) situated at the edges of the leaves. Often the sap seems to be exuded passively along the pathway of least resistance from the vein endings. It is possible that some hydathodes excrete water actively, perhaps following the excretion of solutes (cf. nectaries and salt-glands), but the evidence for this is inconclusive. Many plants in tropical rain forests guttate profusely and to stand beneath some aroids of the genus *Colocasia* is like being out in a gentle drizzle. Guttation is generally more active at night, presumably because the positive pressure in the xylem is highest at the time when transpiration is least.

There has recently been a suggestion (PLUMB and BRIDGMAN, 1972) that gel-like material deposited in the walls of the xylem elements may contribute to the lowered water potential of xylem sap by a reduction in matric potential and that this may be important in the ascent of sap. (For some comments on these ideas see PLUMB and BRIDGMAN, 1973.)

6.7 Transport of water in the phloem

Research on phloem transport has been concerned very largely with the movement of sucrose and little attention has been given to the transport of other solutes or of water. According to the mechanism proposed by MÜNSCH (1930), usually known now as the pressure flow mechanism (Fig. 6–9), sucrose is accumulated in sieve tubes at a 'source' such as a leaf and this causes the osmotic uptake of water and an increase in turgidity. At another place 'the sink', e.g. in the roots, sucrose is unloaded and this leads to an efflux of water and reduced turgidity. Thus there is a gradient

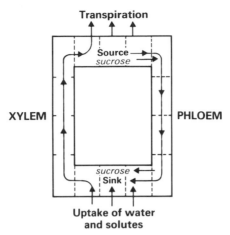

Fig. 6–9   Circulation of water in plants according to the ideas of Münsch. For discussion of this concept, see text.

of hydrostatic pressure between source and sink which will cause a mass flow of water and dissolved substances along the tube. Münsch suggested that water is taken from the xylem at the source and returned to it at the sink so that there is a circulation of water via xylem and phloem. In order that water can be transferred from xylem to phloem in a leaf the water potential of the sieve tube sap must be lower than that of the nearby xylem. Sieve tube sap has a maximum osmotic potential of about -1100 kPa (based on a 10% sucrose solution), and, if the sieve tubes are turgid as they usually are, the water potential will be appreciably less than this. Thus it is difficult to see how water can be transferred into the phloem from the xylem or surrounding cells in a rapidly transpiring leaf which may have a water potential of -2000 kPa or lower. Conversely, at the sink, water will be withdrawn from the phloem only if the water potential of the sieve tube sap is higher (i.e. less negative) than that of the xylem sap (Fig. 6–9).

A number of attempts have been made to demonstrate the transport of water in phloem using the same techniques, e.g. the use of tritium-labelled water and transmission of a heat pulse, as have been used successfully in the case of xylem (p. 91). The results have been disappointing, to say the least, and this together with a number of other considerations has led some investigators e.g. CLEMENTS, 1940, CANNY, 1973, and SUTCLIFFE and COLLINS, 1975, to the view that transport of solutes in the phloem may not be obligatorily dependent on water movement and can occur even in its absence. The best evidence that water moves in the phloem comes from the observation that prolonged exudation sometimes occurs when sieve tubes are cut or pierced by aphid stylets. However, this only proves that the sieve-tube sap is under pressure and that this pressure can be sustained for a considerable period presumably by maintenance of a water-potential gradient through accumulation of solutes in the system.

Despite the difficulty of demonstrating it clearly there is little doubt that some water does move through sieve tubes on occasions at a rate which is determined by existing water-potential gradients and the resistances to flow. It is generally assumed that most of the water that enters a fruit such as a melon during its growth is transported through the phloem but the relative contributions of phloem and xylem have never been accurately assessed. In contrast to transport between roots and leaves this is a situation in which movement through phloem and xylem is in the same direction, (cf. Fig. 6–9).

6.8 Effects of water stress on physiological processes

Water stress occurs when loss of water exceeds absorption. Most plants are subjected to a degree of water stress during the day and the situation is restored at night (see Chapter 5). The presence of water reserves within cell vacuoles or in the xylem enables a plant to withstand severe water stress for a time but obviously an excess of water loss over absorption cannot be tolerated indefinitely.

Plants respond to reduced water supply or excessive transpiration by closure of the stomata. This is brought about by synthesis of abscisic acid in the wilting leaves (see Chapter 4). If this results in a reduction of water stress and the leaves recover their turgidity ABA levels gradually fall and the stomata open normally again after a few days. While the stomata are closed photosynthesis is prevented and growth eventually stops as a result. There are some reports that translocation of sugar in the phloem is reduced under conditions of water stress but in wheat and some other grasses this is apparently not the case, at least for a time. Respiration also slows down with the onset of water stress as oxygen deficiencies develop following closure of the stomata, but often it increases later especially when the stomata open in severely wilted leaves. Some succulent plants, e.g. *Kalanchoe*, show Crassulacean Acid Metabolism only under conditions of water stress and photosynthesize like other plants when abundant water is available. Another effect of water stress is to increase the rate of hydrolysis of starch to sugar and of proteins to amino acids which tends to lower the water potentials of cells and increases their ability to retain water.

If a leaf does not recover its turgidity fairly quickly after closure of the stomata it withers and falls off. Under conditions of severe stress a plant may lose all its leaves except those near the tips of shoots. Meristems are often the most drought resistant parts of a plant because they are able to retain moisture longest. In trees which shed their leaves during periods of drought, or extreme cold when water is frozen and unavailable, the young leaves are protected by bud scales – the main purpose of which is to reduce water loss. In many perennial herbaceous plants all the above ground parts die at times of water stress and the plant survives by underground storage organs such as roots, rhizomes or bulbs.

The growth of trees is controlled more by water availability than by any other environmental factor except perhaps temperature (see SUTCLIFFE, 1977). The effect of climate, and particularly of rainfall on the width of annual rings has provided a basis for the dating of old timber. The science of dendrochronology, as it is called, together with other evidence, has made it possible recently to date accurately for the first time the historic round table in Winchester which has long been associated with the legendary King Arthur and his Knights.

References

ALLAWAY, W. G. (1973). *Planta,* 110, 63–76.

ANDERSSON, N. E., HERTZ, C. H. and RUHFERT, H. (1954). *Physiologia Pl.,* 7, 753–67.

ARBER, A. (1925). *Water Plants. A Study of Aquatic Angiosperms.* University Press, Cambridge.

ARISZ, W. H., HELDER, R. J. and VAN DIE, J. (1951). *J. exp. Bot.,* 2, 257–97.

ARNON, D. I., STOUT, P. R. and SIPOS, F. (1940). *Am. J. Bot.,* 27, 791–8.

BANGE, G. G. J. (1953). *Acta bot. Neerl.,* 2, 255–97.

BENNET-CLARK, T. A., GREENWOOD, A. D. and BARKER, J. W. (1936). *New Phytol.,* 35, 277–91.

BERNAL, J. D. (1965). In *The State and Movement of Water in Living Organisms.* Ed. G. E. Fogg, University Press, Cambridge, 17–32.

BOEHM, J. (1892). *Ber. dt. bot. Ges.,* 48, 109–18.

BOWLING, D. J. F. (1976). *Nature (London),* 262, 393.

BRAUNER, L. (1930). *Ber. dt. bot. Ges.,* 48, 109–18.

BRIGGS, L. J. and SHANTZ, H. L. (1916). *J. agric. Res.,* 7, 155–213.

BROWN, H. T., and ESCOMBE, F. (1900). *Phil. Trans. R. Soc. Ser. B,* 193, 223–91.

BURSTRÖM, H. G. (1971a). *Nature (London),* 234, 488.

BURSTRÖM, H. G. (1971b). *Endeavour,* XXX, 87–90.

CANNY, M. J. (1973). *Phloem Transport.* University Press, Cambridge.

CLARKSON, D. T. (1974). *Ion Transport and Cell Structure in Plants.* McGraw-Hill, Maidenhead.

CLEMENTS, H. F. (1940). *Pl. Physiol.,* 15, 689–700.

DAINTY, J. (1963). *Protoplasma,* 57, 220–8.

DAINTY, J. and GINZBERG, B. Z. (1964). *Biochim. Biophys. Acta,* 79, 102–11.

DARWIN, F. (1898). *Phil. Trans. R. Soc. Ser. B,* 190, 531–621.

DARWIN, F. and PERTZ, D. F. M. (1911). *Phil. Trans. R. Soc. Ser. B,* 84, 136–154.

DELF, E. M. (1911). *Ann. Bot.,* (Old Series), 25, 485–505.

DIXON, H. (1914). *Transpiration and the Ascent of Sap.* Macmillan, London.

EDWARDS, M. and MEIDRER, H. (1975). *J. exp. Bot.,* 26, 319–30.

FALK, S. O. (1966). *Zeitschrift Pfanzenphysiologie,* 55, 31–7.

FISCHER, R. A. and HSIAO, T. C. (1968). *Pl. Physiol.,* 43, 1953.

FISHER, J. C. (1948). *J. appl. Physiol.,* 19, 1062–7.

FRANKS, F. and GOOD, W. (1966). *Nature (London),* 210, 85–6.

FREEMAN G. F. (1908). *Bot. Gaz.,* 46, 118–29.

FUJINO, M. (1967) *Scientific Bulletin of the Faculty of Education,* Nagasaki University, 18, 1–47.

GAFF, D. F. (1971). *Science, N.Y.,* 174, 1033–4.

GEMMELL, A. R. (1969). *Developmental Plant Anatomy.* Studies in Biology, no. 15. Edward Arnold, London.

GREEN, P. B. and STANTON, F. W. (1967). *Science, N.Y.,* 155, 1675–6.

GROSSENBACHER, K. A. (1939). *Am. J. Bot.,* 26, 107–9.

HALES, S. (1727). *Vegetable Staticks.* 1961 edition. Macdonald, London.

HALL, A. E. and KAUFMANN, M. R. (1975). *Pl. Physiol.,* 55, 455–9.

HANDLEY, W. R. C. (1939). *Ann. Bot. (New Series),* 3, 803–12.

HANES, C. S. (1940). *Nature (London)*, **145**, 348.

HARNED, H. S. and OWEN, B. B. (1957). *The Physical Chemistry of Electrolytic Solutions*. 3rd Edition. Reinhold, New York.

HEATH, O. V. S. and ORCHARD, B. (1957). *Nature (London)*, 180, 180–1.

HOFFMAN, G. J. and RAWLINGS, S. L. (1972). *Science, N.Y.*, 177, 802–3.

HUBER, B. (1953). *Forstwissenschaften Zentralblatt*, 72, 257–64.

HUBER, B. and SCHMIDT, E. (1937). *Ber. dt. bot. Ges.*, 55, 514.

HUMBLE, G. D. and RASCHKE, K. (1971). *Pl. Physiol.*, 48, 447–53.

IDLE, D. B. (1976). *Ann. Bot.* (New Series), 40, 473–7.

KAMIYA, N. and TAZAWA, M. (1956). *Protoplasma*, 46, 394–422.

KRAMER, P. J. (1969) *Plant and Soil Water Relationships: A Modern Synthesis*. McGraw-Hill, New York.

KRAMER, P. J., KNIPING, E. B. and MILLER, L. N. (1966). *Science, N.Y.*, 153, 889–90.

KNIGHT, R. C. (1915). *New Phytol.*, 14, 212–16.

KURTZMANN, R. H. (1966). *Pl. Physiol.*, 41, 641–6.

LEVITT, J. (1947). *Pl. Physiol.*, 22, 514–25.

LIVINGSTON (1906). *The Relation of Desert Plants to Soil Moisture and to Evaporation*. Carnegie Institute, Washington Publication, 50, Washington.

LLOYD, F. E. (1908). *The Physiology of Stomata*. Carnegie Institute, Washington Publication, 82. Washington.

MACALLUM, A. B. (1905). *J. Physiol, Lond.*, 32, 95.

MACDOUGAL, D. T. (1925), Carnegie Institute, Washington Publication, 365, Washington.

MANSFIELD, T. A. (1976). *Perspectives in Experimental Biology*. Vol. 2, Botany, 453–62.

MARTIN, E. S. and MEIDNER, H. (1971). *New Phytol.*, 70, 923–8.

MEES, G. C. and WEATHERLEY, P. E. (1957). *Proc. R. Soc. B*, 147, 381–91.

MEIDNER, H. (1965). *School Science Review*, 47, 149–51.

MEIDNER, H. and HEATH, O. V. S. (1959). *J. exp. Bot.*, 10, 206–19.

MEYER, B. S. (1945). *Pl. Physiol.*, 20, 142–64.

MEYER, B. S. and WALLACE, A. M. (1941). *Am. J. Bot.*, 28, 838.

MILBURN, J. (1973). *Planta*, 112, 333–42.

MILLER, E. C. (1938). *Plant Physiology*. 2nd Edition. McGraw-Hill, New York.

MONTEITH, J. L. (1965). In *The State and Movement of Water in Living Organisms*. Ed. G. E. Fogg. University Press, Cambridge.

MÜNSCH, E. (1930). *Die Stoffbewegung in der Pflanze*. Fischer, Jena.

PENMAN, H. L. (1948). *Proc. R. Soc.*, A193, 120–45.

PFEFFER, W. (1877). *Osmotische Untersuchungen*. Engelmann, Leipzig.

PISEK, A. and BERGER, E. (1938). *Planta*, 28, 124–55.

PLUMB, R. C. and BRIDGMAN, W. B. (1972). *Science, N.Y.*, 176, 1129.

PLUMB, R. C. and BRIDGMAN, W. B. et al. (1973). *Science, N.Y.*, 179, 1248–50.

POSTLETHWAITE, S. N. and ROGERS, B. (1958). *Am. J. Bot.*, 45, 753–7.

PRESTON, R. D. (1958). In *Deformation and Flow in Biological Systems*. Ed. A. Frey-Wyssling, 257–331. North Holland Publishing Company, Amsterdam.

RASCHKE, K. and FELLOWS, M. P. (1971). *Planta*, 101, 296–316.

RICHARDS, L. A. (1949). *Soil Science*, 68, 95.

RICHARDSON, M. (1975). *Translocation in Plants*. 2nd Edition. Studies in Biology, no. 10. Edward Arnold, London.

ROBERTS, M. B. V. (1976). *Biology: A Functional Approach*. 2nd Edition. Nelson, London.

ROBINSON, R. A. and STOKES, R. H. (1959). *Electrolytic Solutions.* 2nd Edition. Butterworths, London.

SACHS J. VON (1887). *Lectures of the Physiology of Plants.* English edition. Clarendon Press, Oxford.

SAYRE, J. D. (1926). *Ohio Journal of Science,* 26, 233–67.

SCARTH, J. W. (1932). *Pl. Physiol.,* 7, 481–504.

SCARTH, J. W., LOEWY, A. and SHAW, M. (1948). *Can. J. Res.* C26, 94–107.

SCHOLANDER, P. F., HAMMEL, H. T., BRADSTREET, E. D. and HEMMINGSEN, E. A. (1965). *Science, N.Y.,* 148, 339–46.

SHAW, M. and MACLACHLAN, G. A. (1954). *Can. J. Bot.,* 32, 784–94.

SHIMSHI, D. (1977). *New Phytol.,* 78, 593–8.

SPANNER, D. C. (1951). *J. exp. Bot.,* 2, 145–68.

SPANNER, D. C. (1953). *J. exp. Bot.,* 4, 283–95.

STEPHAN, J. (1881). *Sber. Akad. Wiss. Wien.,* 68, 385.

STILES, W. (1970). *J. appl. Ecol.,* 7, 617–22.

STEUDLE, E. and ZIMMERMANN, U. (1974). *Biochim. biophys Acta,* 332, 399–412.

STOCKING, C. R. (1945). *Am. J. Bot.,* 32, 126–34.

STRASBURGER, E. (1891). *Ueber der Bau und die Verrichtungen der Leitsbahnen in der Pflanzen.* Fischer, Jena.

SUTCLIFFE, J. F. (1977). *Plants and Temperature.* Studies in Biology, no. 86. Edward Arnold, London.

SUTCLIFFE, J. F. and BAKER, D. A. (1974). *Plants and Mineral Salts.* Studies in Biology, no. 48. Edward Arnold, London.

SUTCLIFFE, J. F. and COLLINS, O. D. G. (1975). *Ann. Bot. (New Series),* 40, 627–9.

TAMIYA, H. (1938). *Cytologia (Tokyo),* 8, 542–62.

TRAVIS, A. J. and MANSFIELD, T. A. (1977). *New Phytol.,* 78, 541–6.

VERDUIN, J. (1949). In *Photosynthesis.* Ed. J. Franck and W. E. Loomis. Iowa State College Press, Ames, Iowa.

VILLIERS, T. A. (1975). *Dormancy and Survival in Plants.* Studies in Biology, no. 57. Edward Arnold, London.

WADLEIGH, C. H. and AYERS, A. D. (1945). *Pl. Physiol.,* 20, 106–32.

WEINTRAUB, M. (1952). *New Phytol.,* 50, 357–82.

WILLIAMS, W. T. (1949). *Ann. Bot.* (New Series), 13, 309–27.

WRIGHT, S. T. C. and HIRON, R. W. P. (1969). *Nature (London),* 224, 719–20.

YIN, H. C. and TUNG, Y. T. (1948). *Science, N.Y.,* 108, 87–8.

ZIMMERMANN, M. H. (1965). In *The State and Movement of Water in Living Organisms.* Ed. G. E. Fogg. 151–5. University Press, Cambridge.

ZIMMERMANN, U. and STENDLE, E. (1975). *Aust. J. Pl. Physiol.,* 2, 1–12.

Further Reading

General

FOGG, G. E. (ed.) (1965). *The State and Movement of Water in Living Organisms*. University Press, Cambridge.

KOZLOWSKI, T. T. (1964). *Water Metabolism in Plants*. Harper and Row, New York.

KOZLOWSKI, T. T. (1968–1976). *Water Deficits and Plant Growth*. Vols I–IV. Academic Press, New York and London.

KRAMER, P. J. (1969). *Plant and Soil Water Relationships: A Modern Synthesis*. McGraw-Hill, New York.

SLATYER, R. O. (1967). *Plant-Water Relationships*. Academic Press, London and New York.

Chapter 1

ARBER, A. L. (1925). *Water Plants – A study of Aquatic Angiosperms*. University Press, Cambridge.

DAUBENMIRE, R. F. (1959). *Plants and Environment*. 2nd edition. Wiley, New York.

GEMMELL, A. R. (1969). *Developmental Plant Anatomy*. Studies in Biology, no. 15. Edward Arnold, London.

RANKIAER, C. (1937). *Plant Life Forms*. Translated by H. Gilbert. Clarendon Press, Oxford.

Chapter 2

DICK, D. A. T. (1966). *Cell Water*. Butterworths, London.

EDSALL, J. T. and WYMAN, J. (1958). *Biophysical Chemistry*. Vol. 1. Academic Press, New York.

EISENBERG, D. and KAUZMANN, W. (1969). *The Structure and Properties of Water*. Clarendon Press, Oxford.

NOBEL, P. S. (1974). *Introduction to Biophysical Plant Physiology*. Freeman, San Francisco.

Chapter 3

BOYER, J. S. (1969). Measurement of the water status of plants. *A. Rev. Pl. Physiol.*, **20**, 351–64.

BRIGGS, G. E. (1967). *Movement of Water in Plants*. Blackwells, Oxford.

DAINTY, J. (1969). The water relations of plants. In *Physiology of Plant Growth and Development*. Ed. M. B. Wilkins. McGraw-Hill, New York.

HOUSE, C. R. (1974). *Water Transport in Cells and Tissues*. Edward Arnold, London.

SLAVIK, B. (1974). *Methods of Studying Plant Water Relations*. Chapman and Hall, London.

Chapter 4

ALLAWAY, W. G. and MILTHORPE, F. L. (1976). Structure and functioning of stomata. In Kozlowski T. T. (Ed.) *Water Deficits and Plant Growth*. Vol. IV, 57–102. Academic Press, New York and London.

BURROWS, F. J. and MILTHORPE, F. L. (1976). Stomatal conductance in the control of gas exchange. In Kowlowski, T. T. (Ed.) *Water Deficits and Plant Growth*. Vol. IV, 57–102, 103–52. Academic Press, New York and London.

HEATH, O. V. S. (1959). The water relations of stomatal cells and mechanism of stomatal movement. Chapter 3 in *Plant Physiology – A Treatise*. Ed. F. C. Steward. Vol. II, 193–250, Academic Press, New York and London.

HEATH, O. V. S. (1975). *Stomata*. Oxford Biology Readers, No. 37, Ed. J. L. Head. Oxford University Press, Oxford.

MEIDNER, H. and MANSFIELD, T. A. (1969). *Physiology of Stomata*. McGraw-Hill, New York.

RASCHKE, K. (1975). Stomatal action. *Ann. Rev. Pl. Physiol.*, 26, 309–40.

Chapter 5

KRAMER, P. J. (1959). Transpiration and the water economy of plants. Chapter 7 in *Plant Physiology – A Treatise*. Ed. F. C. Steward. Vol. II, 607–726. Academic Press, New York and London.

MONTEITH, J. L. (1973). *Principles of Environmental Physics*. Edward Arnold, London.

PENMAN, H. L. (1963). *Vegetation and Hydrology*. Technical Communication No. 53, Commonwealth Bureau of Soils, Farnham Royal, England.

RUTTER, A. J. (1972). *Transpiration*. Oxford Biology Readers, No. 24, Ed. J. L. Head and O. E. Lowenstein. Oxford University Press, Oxford.

Chapter 6

BOYER, J. S. (1977). Regulation of water movement in whole plants. In *Integration of Activity in the Higher Plant*. Ed. D. H. Jennings. 455–70. Cambridge University Press, London.

GREENIDGE, K. N. H. (1957). Ascent of sap. *Ann. Rev. Pl. Physiol.*, 11, 237–56.

WEATHERLEY, P. E. (1963). The pathway of water movement across the root cortex and leaf mesophyll of transpiring plants. In *The Water Relations of Plants*. Ed. A. J. Rutter and F. H. Whitehead. 85–100. Blackwells Scientific Publications, Oxford.

ZIMMERMANN, M. H. (1965). Water Movement in stems of tall plants. In *The State and Movement of Water in Living Organisms*. Ed. G. E. Fogg. 151–5. Cambridge University Press, Cambridge.

Glossary

Activation energy: threshold energy required to enable a particle to diffuse, or alternatively to undergo reaction.

Active transport: transport processes that require direct expenditure of metabolic energy.

Adsorption: binding of mobile particles to an immobile material.

Algae: unicellular or multicellular plants of relatively simple structure e.g. *Chlamydomonas* spp., *Nitella* spp., *Valonia* spp. (*q.v.*).

Angiosperms: Plants that form flowers and in which the seeds are enclosed in a fruit.

Anion: negatively charged ion (*q.v.*).

Anti-transpirants: substances that reduce transpiration, usually when sprayed on to the foliage.

Apoplasm: system of inter-connected water-filled spaces in the cell walls of plants.

Atmometer: instrument for measuring the rate of evaporation.

Bryophyta: plants that have a free-living dominant gametophyte stage and a sporophyte stage that is nutritionally dependent on the gametophyte throughout its life. Includes mosses and liverworts.

Bulb: modified shoot consisting of a shortened stem surrounded by a protective coating of scale leaves and leaf bases swollen with food reserves.

Cacti: xerophytic flowering plants in which the leaves are often reduced to spines and the stem enlarged to form the main photosynthetic organ.

Cambium: a zone of meristematic cells (*q.v.*) which gives rise to xylem and phloem (vascular cambium) or to cork (cork cambium).

Capillarity: movement of liquid through narrow channels as a result of surface forces.

Carbohydrates: organic substances containing only carbon, hydrogen and oxygen; the last two in the same proportions as in water.

Casparian band: zone of lipoidal materials in the radial walls of endodermal cells (see suberin).

Cation: positively charged ion (*q.v.*).

Chemical potential: measure of the energy content of particles in a system and therefore of their tendency to diffuse spontaneously from one place to another, or to undergo a reaction.

Circadian rhythm: rhythm with a periodicity of about 24 hours.

Cladode: portion of a stem that is expanded and flattened to form a leaf-like structure.

Coenocyte: multi-nucleate structural unit found in some algae (e.g. *Valonia* spp.) and many fungi.

Collenchyma: Plant cells with irregularly thickened, non-lignified cell walls; found usually near the surface of young stems and leaves and providing mechanical support.

Cork: protective layer of suberized (not lignified) cells formed near the surface of stems and roots as a result of the activity of a cambium (*q.v.*).

Corm: base of a stem which becomes swollen with food reserves and bears buds in the axils of protective scale leaves.

Cortex: outer region of a stem or root, consisting mainly of parenchyma cells (*q.v.*).

Cuticle: impermeable non-cellular layer that covers the surface of leaves and stems of most plants and restricts water loss.

Cytoplasm: all the protoplasm of a cell outside the nucleus.

Cytoplasmic pressure (ψ_c): pressure exerted by the cytoplasm of a plant cell on the vacuolar contents.

Cytoplasmic streaming: circulation of cytoplasm, occurring particularly in some elongated plant cells.

Cytorrhysis: collapse of a cell.

Deciduous: shedding leaves or other parts at a certain season.

Dendrochronology: science of dating wood by study of the annual rings.

Dendrograph: instrument for measuring the diameter of tree trunks.

Dicotyledons: flowering plants with two developed leaves (cotyledons) in the embryo; includes many forest trees, e.g. ash, beech, oak; and crop plants such as peas, beans, cabbage, carrot, potato, etc (cf. monocotyledons).

Dielectric constant: capacity of a substance to displace an electrical charge without flow of current.

Diffusion: random spontaneous movement of particles.

Diffusion pressure deficit (DPD): the amount by which the diffusion pressure of water in a system is less than that of pure water at the same temperature and pressure (cf. water potential difference).

Dissociation: reversible decomposition of an electrolyte in aqueous solution to form ions (*q.v.*); or as a result of heat (thermal dissociation).

Elastic coefficient (ϵ=Young's modulus)*:* ratio of the stress on a material to the longitudinal strain.

Electrolyte: substance that dissociates into ions in aqueous solution.

Electro-osmosis: net diffusion of charged particles in an electrical gradient.

Endodermis: layer of closely-packed cells separating the cortex from the stele in roots and also found in stems of some ferns and some dicotyledons (see Casparian band).

Endoplasmic reticulum: internal cytoplasmic membranes.

Entropy: state of intrinsic stability of a system; the greater its entropy the more stable is the system and the smaller its capacity for spontaneous change.

Epidermis: surface layer of the aerial parts of a plant; some botanists refer to the surface layer of a root as an epidermis, although it is not distinct structurally here as it is in the shoot.

Ferns: (Filicales) plants that have free living gametophyte and sporophyte generations with the sporophyte dominant for most of the life history. Leaves are usually large and conspicuous bearing sporangia on the under surface, and often called fronds.

Fibres: elongated plant cells with pointed ends and lignified cell walls. Found mainly in xylem and phloem (sclerenchyma), they function as mechanical support.

Fungi: non-green plants of relatively simple structure which obtain carbon from organic materials in the environment.

Fungicide: a substance that kills fungi.

Guard cells: modified epidermal cells (usually two) surrounding a stoma and regulating the size of the aperture.

Guttation: excretion of liquid water through 'water-pores' or hydathodes (*q.v.*).

Gymnosperms: cone-bearing seed plants, e.g. pines and firs.

Halophytes: Plants that grow in highly saline conditions.

Heavy water: water containing some deuterium (^2H) or tritium (^3H) atoms.

Herbaceous: not woody.

Herbicide: a substance that kills plants.

Hydathode: glandular structure through which liquid water is excreted, either passively or actively.

Hydraulic conductivity (L_p): permeability of a system to water.

Hydrocarbons: substances composed entirely of hydrogen and carbon.

Hydrophytes: plants that grow submerged, or mainly submerged, in water (cf. hygrophytes).

Hygrometer: instrument for measurement of relative humidity (*q.v.*).

Hygrophytes: plants that grow habitually in very wet soil with their leaves in highly humid air.

Hyper-osmotic (hypertonic): solution of lower, i.e. more negative osmotic potential, i.e. higher osmotic pressure (*q.v.*).

Hypo-osmotic (hypotonic): solution of higher, i.e. less negative osmotic potential i.e. lower osmotic pressure (*q.v.*).

Imbibition: attraction of water by a substance (see matric potential).

Incipient plasmolysis: point at which separation of cell wall and underlying cytoplasm first begins following osmotic withdrawal of water from the vacuole of a plant cell.

Ion: charged particle released on dissociation of an electrolyte in aqueous solution.

Iso-osmotic (isotonic): solutions of equal osmotic potentials (or pressure).

Isotopes: atoms of the same element having the same atomic number but different atomic mass; some decompose spontaneously (radioactive isotopes, e.g. ^{32}P) and others are stable (e.g. ^{18}O).

Latent heat of melting (fusion): amount of heat absorbed when one gram of a substance is converted from the solid to the liquid state at the same temperature.

Latent heat of vaporization: amount of heat absorbed when one gram of a substance is converted from the liquid to the gaseous state at the same temperature.

Lichen: symbiotic association between a fungus and an alga to form a composite plant.

Lignin: complex polymer of various derivatives of phenylpropane; occurring in some plant cell walls, notably in the xylem and in phloem fibres (sclerenchyma), giving them strength rigidity.

Lysimeter: instrument for estimating the amount of water lost from plants.

Matric potential (ψ_m): component of water potential that is due to the presence of particles which attract water.

Meristem: localized region of a plant in which rapid cell division occurs, e.g. near the apex of shoot and root (apical meristem).

Meristematic cells: embryonic cells in a state of rapid cell division.

Mesophyll: Photosynthetic cells in a leaf; usually loosely arranged with large intercellular spaces.

Mesophytes: plants that grow in moist, well aerated soils, with their leaves in moderately dry air.

Monocotyledons: plants with one seed leaf (cotyledon); e.g. grasses, banana, palms (cf. dicotyledons).

Mycorrhizal fungi: Symbiotic fungi associated with the roots of various plants, e.g. pines and beech.

Nitella: genus of aquatic algae in which the cells are unusually large and so are convenient for studies of water and solute relations.

Osmometer: apparatus for demonstrating osmosis or measuring osmotic pressure.

Osmosis: spontaneous movement of a solvent (usually water) from a place where its chemical potential is higher to another where it is lower.

Osmotic potential: (ψ_π): component of water potential that is due to the presence of solute.

Osmotic pressure (π): amount of excess pressure that must be applied to a solution in an osmometer (*q.v.*) when pure water is supplied outside which prevents the entry of water. Numerically equal to osmotic potential, but opposite in sign.

Parenchyma: packing tissue consisting of thin-walled vacuolated cells that makes up the bulk of a plant.

Permanent wilting percentage (*PWP*): water content of a soil (expressed as a percentage of the dry matter) at which the leaves of a test plant growing in it becomes permanently wilted.

Permeability: ease of movement of particles, e.g. molecules or ions, through a system, e.g. a membrane.

pH: acidity (or alkalinity) of a solution expressed as hydrogen ion concentration on a reciprocal logarthimic scale.

Phloem: living tissue through which organic and inorganic substances are transported either upwards or downwards in a plant.

Photosynthesis: conversion of carbon dioxide to organic compounds through the agency of light.

Phyllode: flattened expanded leaf petiole forming a photosynthetic organ (cf. cladode).

Pits: perforations in the walls of lignified plant cells through which run plasmodesmata (*q.v.*).

Planimeter: instrument for measuring area.

Plasma membrane (plasmalemma): outer cytoplasmic membrane of a plant cell, underlying the cell wall.

Plasmodesmata: protoplasmic connections between neighbouring cells.

Plasmolysis: retraction of the cytoplasm from the wall of a vacuolated plant cell as a result of osmotic withdrawal of water from the vacuole.

Poikilohydrous: water content varies in response to environmental conditions (particularly humidity).

Porometer: instrument for measuring the size of stomata (*q.v.*).

Potometer: instrument for measuring water absorption by a plant or plant part.

Pressure potential (ψ_p)*:* component of water potential that is due to hydrostatic pressure (see also wall pressure).

Protoplasm: living material of cells (i.e. cytoplasm + nucleus).

Psychrometer: apparatus for measuring vapour pressure, and hence water potential.

Q_{10} *(temperature coefficient):* the ratio of the rate of a process at a particular temperature over its rate at a temperature 10° C lower.

Reflection coefficient: measure of the extent to which solutes penetrate a plant cell from an external solution.

Refractive index: extent to which a ray of light travelling obliquely is bent (refracted) at a surface separating two media.

Refractometer: instrument for measuring the refractive index of a solution.

Relative humidity (RH): amount of water present in a given volume of air expressed as a percentage of the amount the air can hold at the same temperature.

Respiration: sequence of chemical reactions whereby energy is made available for energy-requiring processes.

Rhizome: underground stem which is often modified as a storage organ.

Root pressure: force developed in the roots, mainly by accumulation of solutes in the xylem sap, which causes water to be forced under pressure upwards in to the stem.

Sieve tubes: specialized cells in the phloem of seed plants which form channels for transport of solutes.

Specific heat: amount of heat required to raise the temperature of one gram of a substance by 1°C.

Starch sheath: Layer of cells, rich in starch, which separates the stele and cortex in stems (cf. endodermis).

Stele: inner region of a stem or root which contains the xylem and phloem and is separated from the outer cortex by the starch-sheath (stem) or endodermis (root).

Stomata: pores through which exchange of gases occurs in the aerial parts of plants.

Stomatal index: a number of stomata expressed as a percentage of the number of epidermal cells per unit of area.

Suberin: complex mixture of lipoidal substances deposited in some cell walls, e.g. in cork tissue, rendering them impervious to water.

Succulents: plants with swollen stems or leaves, e.g. many members of the families Cactaceae and Crassulaceae.

Suction force (*=suction pressure*): force responsible for entry of water into a plant cell (see water potential).

Surface tension: strength with which molecules are attracted to a surface.

Symplasm: inter-connected cytoplasm in a multicellular plant (see also plasmodesmata).

Temperature coefficient: see Q_{10}.

Tensile strength: force required to break a material under tension.

Tensiometer: instrument used for determining the water potential of soil solutions.

Thermal conductivity: ability to conduct heat.

Thermocouple: instrument for measuring temperature, in which an electric current is caused to flow through a bi-metallic junction.

Tonoplast: cytoplasmic membrane bounding the central vacuole of a plant cell.

Total soil-moisture stress (*TSMS*): water potential of soil solution.

Tracheids: spindle-shaped lignified cells that occur in the xylem of all ferns and seed plants and function both as mechanical support and as channels of solution transport.

Transpiration: loss of water from plants by evaporation.

Transpiration stream: solution flowing in the xylem as a result of transpiration.

Tuber: a root or portion of an underground stem that is swollen with food reserves.

Turgidity: firmness of a cell, tissue or organ caused by uptake of water and consequent stretching of the cell wall (see also turgor pressure).

Turgor pressure: pressure exerted by the contents of a plant cell on the cell wall as a result of wall pressure.

Utricularia spp. (*bladderworts*): aquatic angiosperms which have leaves modified to form bladders which trap insects and digest them.

Vacuole: water-filled spaces in cytoplasm, each surrounded by a tonoplast.

Valonia spp: coenocytic marine algae, used in studies of plant water and salt relations.

Vapour pressure (*saturation vapour pressure*): partial pressure exerted by the vapour of a solution when it comes to equilbirium with the liquid phase at a given temperature and external pressure.

Vascular tissue: xylem and phloem.

Vessels: pipe-like structures formed from files of cells in the xylem of most angiosperms and a few ferns, through which water and dissolved substances are transported.

Viscosity: resistance to flow.

Wall pressure: pressure exerted by the stretched cell wall on cell contents (see pressure potential).

Water potential: difference in chemical potential of water in a system and that of pure water at the same temperature and pressure.

Xerophytes: plants that are adapted to grow under dry conditions, e.g. cacti.

Xylem: lignified tissue through which water and dissolved substances are transported upwards in a plant. Often referred to as wood, it consists of vessels (not in gymnosperms and most ferns), tracheids, fibres and parenchyma.

Subject Index

H50 745 293 6